Homes for Living

Homes for Living

FINDING JOY IN THE EVERYDAY

JESSICA HANLEY & REBECCA MASON

piglet in bed

Contents

A NOTE FROM JESSICA, FOUNDER OF PIGLET IN BED — 6
THE MAKINGS OF A PIGLET HOME — 10

The Bedroom — 14
BRINGING COLOUR INTO YOUR BEDROOM — 18
HOW DOES COLOUR AFFECT OUR MOOD? — 20
EATING IN BED ISN'T SLOVENLY, IT'S CHIC — 24
CURRIED CHEESE ON TOAST — 28
LIFE IS TOO SHORT TO IRON YOUR SHEETS — 30
THE ART OF THE PERFECT NAP — 36
OUR TRIED-AND-TESTED 6–10PM WIND-DOWN ROUTINE — 40

The Kitchen — 44
THE GRAVITATIONAL PULL OF THE KITCHEN — 46
THE MUGS THAT TELL A STORY — 52
ON COLOUR-CODING AND OTHER KITCHEN CRIMES — 54
WHY THE BRITISH ARE SO GOOD AT COMFORT FOOD — 58
THE ULTIMATE CHICKEN PIE — 60
BROCCOLI SOUP WITH STILTON CROUTONS — 66
POTATOES: A PIGLET RANKING — 70
CREAMED CORN AND TUNA JACKET POTATOES — 74

The Living Room — 76
A ROOM FOR LIVING IN — 78
A GUIDE TO THE PERFECT 'PICKY BITS' PLATE — 82
THE NOOK: CREATING SPACE FOR HOBBIES — 84
THE JOY OF REARRANGING — 90
WELCOMING THE OUTSIDE IN — 92
HOW TO COLLECT AND DISPLAY ART IN YOUR HOME — 96

The Bathroom   100
MAKING A SPLASH IN THE BATHROOM   104
HOW TO BE USELESS TO EVERYONE: TAKE A LONG BATH   108
THE HUMBLEBRAG THAT IS THE DOWNSTAIRS LOO   114

The Garden   120
GROWING THINGS: WHY DOES IT MAKE US SO HAPPY?   122
THE LOST ART OF PICNICKING   128
SPINACH AND FETA ROLLS   136
SMOKED AUBERGINE DIP   138
HOW TO MAKE THE MOST OF SUPERMARKET HERBS   142

Hosting   144
HOSTING, BUT MAKE IT CHILL   148
HOW TO CREATE A GREAT TABLESCAPE   152
TABLE NAPKINS: THREE WAYS   162
HOW TO MAKE CHRISTMAS WORTH THE EFFORT   164
SQUASH, WALNUT AND CHEDDAR PITHIVIER   172
POTATO RÖSTIS WITH SMOKED SALMON AND CRÈME FRAÎCHE   174
SUSTAINABLE GIFT-WRAP IDEAS   176

A FINAL WORD FROM JESSICA   180
INDEX   182
ACKNOWLEDGEMENTS   186
ABOUT THE AUTHORS   188

A note from Jessica, founder of Piglet in Bed

When I think about my childhood, I often picture myself dozing off on the sofa in our little sitting room in West London. My legs up on my mum's lap, my sister Rebecca reading in one armchair and my dad in the other, maybe talking over some historical documentary on the television. In the colder months, when the fire was often on, our heavy patterned curtains worked hard to keep out the draught. I felt so warm and cosy surrounded by my family. It was repetitive and unexceptional, and I loved it. The pressures that came with chronically underperforming at school seemed to melt away in our little nest.

When I grew up and moved out, I began exploring different versions of 'home'. First, I lived in a dingy party flat in West London that was as hedonistic as it was mouldy. I then moved to East London, revelling in the wave of bars, restaurants and music that were on every street corner at the time. My next stop was the Middle East, living in fairly characterless but objectively swanky flats in Beirut and Dubai.

It took living abroad for six years for me to really appreciate what I had grown up with and how the UK's weather, food, countryside, history and character would shape how I wanted to live my life and the business I would build.

Meanwhile, I was learning about what excited me professionally as the businesses that I admired were being transformed by social media. Expressions of authenticity and joy were replacing the polished and aspirational brands that I had grown up with. Women were rejecting the idea that they should be told by corporations how to behave, how to look and how to dress – but I couldn't help feeling that homewares were falling behind. The interiors that I was seeing in catalogues and showrooms didn't reflect how I was living (for instance it had never occurred to me to iron my sheets!) or what felt important to me in how I created a home.

Piglet in Bed was born out of the desire to capture the feeling of love and comfort that I had experienced in my childhood home, to celebrate the imperfections of our authentic lives, and to enable people to express themselves rather than pressuring them to conform. Linen was the wonder fabric I started with because not only is it sustainably produced but it also innately embodies the low-maintenance and effortless look I was hoping to achieve.

In 2017, I moved in with my mum, who by this point was living in rural West Sussex. With her help, I filled our shed with linen duvet covers and pillowcases, launched Piglet's website and started sending out our first orders from the village post office. Every time we received an order, our phones would let us know with a loud 'ka-ching' sound that would give us the wave of excitement and adrenaline we needed to keep going until the next one came in. Even back then, when the business was tiny, I felt like we were creating something new and heartfelt that we could feel proud of.

A lot has changed since then. Our team works not from a shed but from an office in London. We've expanded into lots of new product categories, discovered how important pattern and the ability to mix and match is to our offering, grown a large US business and a wonderful community of followers online.

Nowadays I live in the US with my American husband Patrick and our two sons. While I love our life here, I sometimes feel that sense of homesickness that originally inspired the creation of Piglet in Bed. It offers me a romantic lens through which I can see what makes our country and our idea of home so unique and so alluring. In many ways, Piglet in Bed is a celebration of everything and everyone I miss so much.

This book is an attempt to bottle the essence of Piglet in Bed. We will guide you room by room through a house of our own imagining, in which comfort, authenticity and beauty meet. Throughout its pages you will find inspiration to help you create a home in which you can truly relax, and ideas for how to slow life down. You will see how we use colour, pattern and texture to achieve spaces that look beautiful yet feel laid-back, and discover how light, sound, scent and other elements of the natural world contribute to our wellbeing. You'll also find a handful of deliciously simple recipes for all occasions, and hear about some of the fun ways we weave joy into our lives every day. We hope you will find inspiration from the pages of this book and apply them in your own unique way to your home. None of the guidance is prescriptive, and most of the tips and advice can be applied large or small, on any budget.

I couldn't think of a better person to help me to capture some of the warmth and fun that fills a Piglet home than my sister Rebecca, who shares every reference and memory that I've poured into the business. She may be quite a lot tidier than me and we don't entirely align on our philosophy regarding dogs on beds, but bringing together the essays in this book has reminded us of just how similar we really are.

With love,

Jessica

The makings of a Piglet home

At Piglet in Bed, when we think of home we think of family, in all its wonderful and diverse forms, and of a place where we can truly be ourselves, a place of safety and refuge from external pressures. You will find the themes of comfort, individuality and authenticity threaded through the stories in this book, as they go to the very heart of Piglet in Bed. We always try to keep the following principles in mind.

NO TWO HOMES NEED BE THE SAME

A home should reflect the personalities and lifestyles of those who live there. Just as our childhood bedrooms revealed our passions and interests of the time, so should our adult homes. While we may no longer be displaying our sports-day trophies or Blu-Tacking posters of bands onto the walls, the idea remains the same. Surround yourself with things that reflect who you are and don't worry about trends. A set of prescriptive rules on how you should live in your home would be to the detriment of individuality, so, with all of our ideas and suggestions, take from them only what speaks to you.

COMFORT IS EVERYTHING

Comfort is the true key to making your house a home. It is the tree that bears the best fruit: security, familiarity and contentment. We will speak a lot in these pages about warmth, wellbeing and cosiness, all concepts that fall under the umbrella of comfort. Don't fall into the trap of wanting your rooms to look like they belong in a Dubai hotel. Sofas should be squishy, cushions don't need to be artfully arranged and crockery can be chipped.

CHOOSE NATURAL MATERIALS THAT LAST

The benefits of natural fibres over synthetic ones are numerous, but first and foremost are their sustainability credentials. Materials such as cotton, linen and wool are derived from plants and animals: renewable resources that can be replenished through sustainable farming and grazing practices. They decompose naturally in the environment, unlike synthetic fibres such as polyester and nylon that remain in landfill for generations.

Fabrics made from natural sources are highly durable and wonderfully low-maintenance. They offer warmth and texture, without compromising their appearance. Linen and wool in particular allow ideal temperature regulation, being both breathable and insulating at the same time.

The material composition of what we bring into our home is the first thing we consider when buying anything new. We want to invest in items with a timeless beauty that will soften, rather than wear out, with age.

DOES IT SERVE A PURPOSE OR BRING YOU JOY?

As William Morris famously said, 'Have nothing in your house that you do not know to be useful, or believe to be beautiful.' When bringing anything new into your home, ask yourself whether it has a practical use. If not, does its presence give you a positive feeling? To quote Marie Kondo, does it 'spark joy'? For most of us, the items in our home are always competing for space, so when making a new purchase or bringing anything new into the house, consider purpose as well as aesthetics. Light those expensive candles and enjoy them, rather than letting them gather dust on the shelf. Buy books that you are genuinely interested in. Keep the lamp that doesn't really go with the rest of the room, because it reminds you of the time you thrifted it over a decade ago for your first flat.

THINGS BECOME MORE BEAUTIFUL WITH LOVE

It is worth thinking about how pieces in your home will age. Will they stand the test of time and withstand wear and tear from various family members or will everyday life prove too much for them? We love seeing the effects of a life well lived: door knobs shiny with use, tabletops bearing the faint scars of water marks and pen indentations, a sofa slightly sagging in the middle from evenings spent lounging. Enjoy the imperfections, cracks and scuffs that come with life and allow your home to reflect them.

ENJOY THE IMPERFECT

We are bombarded with images of perfect homes, with not a bit of clutter in sight. Some of these homes seem to be in a constant state of beautification, with 'before and after' room reveals coming in fast and strong. We need to lower our expectations of what 'normal' looks like and stop working towards a finished tableau when it comes to where we live. Just as life marches on, messy, full and sometimes chaotic, so should your home.

'We love seeing the effects of a life well lived.'

The Bedroom

Bringing colour into your bedroom

Your bedroom is the perfect canvas on which to express your personality. It is a room that is truly yours – no one else has to like it. Using colour is a versatile way of putting your own stamp on a room and has the advantage of being changeable; repainting the walls or switching up your fabrics is something that can have a huge impact on how your space feels.

COLOUR DRENCHING

Colour drenching is a bold interior design technique where a single colour is used across multiple elements of a room, such as the wall, ceiling and textiles. It creates an intentional, cohesive effect across a space.

A way to break up the colour and to avoid the look becoming too 'blocky' is to use multiple shades of the same colour. For example, if you were colour drenching your room in a dark green, you might want to bring in some sage or lighter green accents. This way you don't lose the dramatic effect but it does provide interest to the eye.

MIXING PATTERNS

We love mixing patterns and find it very effective when creating a cosy space that feels eclectic and considered at the same time. The key to combining patterns is, you guessed it, colour! Choose patterns that share a common colour – this doesn't have to be immediately obvious. A small bit of colour in a floral design will be picked out subtly by a fabric of the same colour, for example.

Mix pattern types. Rather than choosing a blue gingham and a yellow gingham together, choose a blue gingham and a floral that discreetly picks up the same blue in the pattern. Organic patterns (florals, paisleys), geometric patterns (checks, plaids or stripes) and textural patterns (herringbone, pinstripe) can work well together, especially when combined under a considered colour scheme.

When pattern mixing, the use of solid colours can provide a 'palette-cleanser' to avoid the look from becoming overly chaotic.

'Choose patterns that share a common colour.'

How does colour affect our mood?

Colour can have a psychological impact and affect our mood, emotions and behaviour. Warm colours, such as red and orange, are known to energise; cool colours like blue and green calm and soothe; neutrals provide balance. While colour theory can prove helpful when working out what colours work well together and how to mix and match, choosing the right colour for your bedroom is really about how it makes you feel.

While some people find blue a peaceful and soothing colour, others might find it cold. A sunny yellow might feel bright and cheery for some but too intense for others. When looking at rooms for inspiration, take note of which ones make you feel uplifted, or peaceful, or happy, and try to find the common factor among them. More often than not you will notice a colour theme running throughout the ones you are drawn to.

Once you have an idea of the colours you want to feature in your bedroom, what remains is figuring out how to incorporate them. Here are a few ideas:

BUT WHAT IF YOU'RE A NEUTRALS PERSON?

Colour drenching and pattern mixing might just not be for you. Colour can be overstimulating and your bedroom might be crying out for something neutral. In many ways, choosing neutrals can be a more challenging exercise than colour. We would recommend painting large swatches on the wall and seeing how the colour responds to the light throughout the day. It is amazing how many shades of off-white there are and how different they can look when painted onto the wall.

One way to create interest within a neutral palette is to incorporate different textures. Linen curtains with a coarse texture can add so much depth to a space. A neutral fabric with a subtle striped texture can elevate your bedding to something much more interesting.

FOLLOW YOUR INSTINCTS

Remember that you'll spend (at least) a third of your life in your bedroom, so follow your instincts and if you don't like it, change it. Piglet founder Jess once painted all the walls in her bedroom a dark blue and found that she was wanting to spend less and less time in it. Objectively, it looked good, but it wasn't making her feel good. After living with the mistake for months she woke up one morning and decided to repaint it a much lighter blue. Suddenly it felt like her space again. Don't be afraid to be bold and don't be afraid to change things that aren't right.

Eating in bed isn't slovenly, it's chic

When we were children, we once asked our grandmother why she never had breakfast in bed. Unlike us, she had no school to get up for, she lived in her own house and made her own rules. We simply couldn't understand why she wouldn't take her tea and toast to bed and get back under the warm covers. She looked at us in horror. 'Just imagine the crumbs, darlings!' She shuddered at the thought. For her, breakfast in bed meant that your standards had slipped to a point of no return or that you were desperately ill.

We laughed off her reaction and remained adamant that, on this point at least, she was quite wrong. Where Granny saw slobbery, we saw luxury. We had never stayed in a hotel until we were well into our teens and we used to discuss the concept of room service in awestruck tones. 'So, apparently, you call someone on the phone and order food, like in a restaurant, and then they bring it to your door on a tray.' Even now, as fully fledged adults, ordering room service feels massively indulgent.

Let's remind ourselves of the second Piglet principle of valuing comfort above all else and shake off the generational puritanism. We can put a chic new spin on eating in bed. Think less 'doomscrolling in stale sheets with your hand in a grab bag of salt and vinegar crisps' and more 'light a candle, open the curtains and put your crisps in a bowl'. To make in-bed dining an act of delicious indulgence you need to do it with intention and set the scene:

- Straighten the bed. Unfluffed pillows, tangled sheets, duvets that are all puffy at the bottom and down-less at the top – no thanks.

- Decide what media you are going to consume, because no-one snacks in bed just to stare at the wall. Get the TV show primed and ready to go or find the right page in your book. People now have stands on which to put their Kindles and use remote controls to avoid having to turn the pages of their e-books: this is the level of laziness that we should all aspire to.

- Let in some natural light where you can, make the room smell nice and never, ever turn on the big light.

- Consider your receptacles. Dry roasted peanuts out of the bag: dusty, greasy, aeroplane snack. Dry roasted peanuts in a pretty little bowl: refined, luxury, protein-rich.

There are no rules regarding what you eat. A twenty-scoop bowl of ice cream like Kevin McCallister in *Home Alone*? Delightful. An entire pizza, dripping with cheese? Yes. A plate of shucked oysters? Delicious, maybe, but probably a step too far for us. We don't think this would have convinced Granny, but she would also have been completely baffled by the concept of loungewear, so we can all agree that some things do change for the better.

Curried cheese on toast

SERVES 1
COOK TIME: 10 MINUTES

¼ red onion, peeled and finely sliced
½ lemon
1 tsp cumin seeds
1 tsp coriander seeds
1 tsp nigella seeds
50g mature Cheddar
¼ green chilli
1 tbsp vegetable oil
1 tbsp mild curry powder
½ tsp ground turmeric
2 slices of sourdough bread
a few coriander leaves

You'll need a plate, but be brave and take this spicy cheese on toast right back to bed with you. It makes for a punchy breakfast or late-night snack.

1. Put the onion into a small bowl, squeeze over the lemon juice and scrunch up with your hands. Leave to pickle for at least 15 minutes, mixing with a spoon from time to time.

2. Put a small frying pan over a medium heat, add the cumin seeds and coriander seeds and toast for 1 minute, then tip them into a pestle and mortar and bash them to break them up a bit. Tip them into a small mixing bowl, along with the nigella seeds.

3. Grate the Cheddar and finely chop the chilli, then add these to the bowl with the spices.

4. Add the oil to the frying pan over a medium heat, then add the curry powder and turmeric. Cook for about 30 seconds, then tip into the bowl and give everything a good mix.

5. Heat your grill to high. Pop the bread on a small baking tray and grill for 2 minutes until golden.

6. Flip the bread over. Spoon the spiced cheese mixture on top of both slices, then return to the grill for 2–3 minutes until the cheese is melted, bubbly and golden.

7. Get your cheese on toast on a plate, then spoon over some of the pickled red onions and some coriander leaves. Take your plate off to bed.

Life is too short to iron your sheets

As we grow older, our pot of free time becomes more and more depleted, while our desire to do more with it increases. In childhood, there are vast chasms of time to fill, a great deal of which are spent generally mooching around in various poses of ennui and sighing dramatically at how terribly boring life is (just us?). Tragically, this is teamed with a total lack of desire to take up hobbies, learn a musical instrument or take the dog for a walk. We remember complaining as children of being bored. 'Bored?!' our mother would say. 'Oh, how I would love to be bored.' At the time we thought she was being dramatic (sorry Mum) but of course now we realise she was just being truthful.

As adults, we can think of countless ways to fill our time, some creative and life-enriching and some … not so much (reality TV is a cruel mistress). The trick seems to be learning how to prioritise things in the order of how much they will ultimately make your life better.

It is all too easy to drown in mundane tasks that rob us of the time to do the things that we really care about and live by standards that exist nowhere apart from in our heads. No one wants 'immaculately folded clothes' engraved on their tombstone.

And so we come to ironing bedsheets. This is part of the mental ballast that we can consciously decide to let go of as life gets busier and fuller. It turns out that slightly crumpled bedsheets don't look any worse. In fact, we would say that that they are softer and more inviting. The whole family is more likely to pile into an imperfectly made bed in the middle of the day than a starched, tucked-in one that you could bounce a coin on.

When you start letting go and freeing up the hours previously spent on attaining perfection, what rushes in is warmth and joy. It is a constant exercise in reshuffling your priorities. So don't be sucked into ironing your bedsheets just because you feel you should.

'When you start letting go, what rushes in is warmth and joy.'

The art of the perfect nap

The concept of Piglet in Bed started with knowing the value of rest and good sleep. Sleeping in a peaceful environment, under natural, breathable fabrics, is the first building block to your overall wellbeing. We would like to spare a thought for the Daytime Nap: less talked about than its far more famous sibling, A Good Night's Sleep, and much more indulgent.

People for whom sleeping in the day is a struggle often sneer at those of us who love a nap. They say it's a waste of time or that they won't be able to sleep at night or that (and it pains us even to say it) sleep is for the weak. To this we say, with love and the deepest respect, jog on. If you don't love a little nap from time to time, then you are probably doing it wrong.

When planning a quick lie-down, grabbing forty winks, having a little napperoony, we must think of the following:

TIME OF DAY

The optimal time to have a nap is in the middle of the afternoon, between 1–3pm. This is usually when you experience the biggest dip in your energy levels and the thought of being horizontal in bed is the most appealing. An early-afternoon nap is least likely to interfere with your night-time sleep and will give you a boost in energy to keep you going until bedtime. The only exception to this is the disco nap, which is best taken in late afternoon to prepare you for a long and fun-filled night out. It is an excellent nap to have in the repertoire and one that has served us well over the years.

LOCATION

Location will depend on your level of commitment to the nap. In bed, under the covers, with the curtains drawn, shows maximum commitment to sleep and signals to others in the house that this is a survival nap and must not be disturbed. A sofa nap has the advantage of being spontaneous, with an added bonus of comfort if the television or radio is making soothing, low-level chatter in the background.

DURATION

The 20-minute power nap is the nap that gets the most press, celebrated for its brevity and energy-boosting properties. Nap purists would argue that, while effective, it doesn't provide quite the same level of cosiness and comfort that a longer nap would. Anything up to 60 minutes allows more rest than a power nap without entering into a deep sleep phase, which can leave you groggy. A full sleep-cycle nap is about 90 minutes and allows for both deep and light sleep. It can improve memory, creativity and mood, though finding a spare hour and a half of an afternoon can be challenging to say the least.

THE GOLDEN RULES

Napping is serious business. Follow these golden rules to being a good napper and you can't go wrong:

1. Nap with pride and don't be persuaded to 'just push through'.

2. Choose your nap judiciously based on the time you have versus your level of sleepiness.

3. Don't be grumpy when you wake up. It cancels out the joy of the nap and will make everyone resent you for it.

4. Remember your essentials: cosy accessories are a must for the experienced napper. Reach for the item that, by its very presence, encourages sleep, whether it's the cool side of your favourite pillow, the comfort of a chunky blanket or a soft throw hung on the back of the sofa.

Our tried-and-tested 6–10pm wind-down routine

There are nights when 'getting ready for bed' consists of kicking your shoes into a corner of the room, adding your clothes to the chair-drobe of doom and brushing your teeth for a cursory 30 seconds. If you're feeling extra conscientious you might remove your makeup. There are also nights when the routine starts at 6pm. On those nights you are dedicated to the task, you are gifting your body and mind some time to wind down and get ready for a good night's sleep. These two versions of ourselves can co-exist perfectly happily, but when we are feeling more like the latter, this is how we do it:

6–6.30pm

- Finish the email, close the laptop.

- It is time to move our bodies, especially if we have been sitting at a desk for most of the day. This is a great time to go for a walk, especially in the lighter months. A half-hour gentle stroll in the fresh air enables our brains to transition from work to relaxation mode.

6.30–7.30pm

- Dinner prep and eat. We have usually been looking forward to dinner from the moment we finished lunch and so are likely to have something in mind to prepare when we get back from our walk.

- After dinner, wash the dishes and wipe down the surfaces. Never leave this until the next day – the 'you' of tomorrow will always be so grateful. We like to think of this as 'closing up the kitchen' for the night, ready for the breakfast service in the morning.

7.30–8.30pm

- Now that you've moved your body and fed it, let's pamper it. This might take the form of a bath or an 'everything shower' but either way, invest some time in it and really wallow. Cleanse, oil, buff and hydrate your skin until you are glowing like a little shiny piglet.

- If ever there was a time for fresh pyjamas, it is now. Choose your comfiest set and pull on some soft, warm socks.

8.30–10pm

- This is your time to read, journal or watch your favourite TV show: if you can do this from bed, even better. Try to limit phone usage during this time in order to keep your mind from day-to-day pressures and avoid too much blue light.

- At 10pm, turn off your light. Hopefully the night will be long and restful and you will wake up the next morning recharged and ready to face the day.

'Sleeping in a peaceful environment, under natural, breathable fabrics, is the first building block of your wellbeing.'

The Kitchen

The gravitational pull of the kitchen

If you are having lots of people round, don't bother turning on the lights in the sitting room: no one will be in there. Instead, everyone will be squashed together in the kitchen, shouting over the music and keeping within an arm's length of the island. Why? It's got all the booze, all the food and all the vibes.

Alfred Hitchcock said that 'happiness is a small house, with a big kitchen'. While we wouldn't normally associate the Master of Suspense with a cosy night in, he nevertheless makes a good point. Back in the day, when families might have had a dedicated dining room, a 'kitchen supper' was synonymous with informality and day-to-day living. If you were invited for a kitchen supper, you were essentially part of the family.

Why is it that we are so drawn to the kitchen? As humans, when gathering, we seek three things: warmth, sustenance and company. The kitchen usually has all three. By virtue of it housing the oven and the stove, the kitchen will nearly always be the warmest room of the house. If you are milling around the kitchen, the chances are that food will be offered at some point. You wouldn't, after all, want to miss the biscuit tin being handed round.

The main draw, however, is company. Kitchen company is a commitment-light way of being around people but with limited social obligation. You can sit in the corner of the kitchen and read your book, or do your homework at the kitchen table, or prepare the dinner without having to make huge amounts of conversation if you don't want to. The kitchen is a space where everyone can get on with what they want, allow the chatter of the house to wash over them and engage when they feel drawn to, all in the most relaxing manner.

At parties, the kitchen has the advantage of the fridge and having lots of surface area for resting drinks. It's informal, it's loud and it's full of life. The kitchen is where you have big family arguments and it is where you resolve them, usually over food. It is the place of impromptu kitchen discos, board game fiascos and dinners with friends stretching into the night while candle wax drips onto the table.

We always think of functionality first, when it comes to the kitchen, but let's also remember that if you are able to make this not only a workable space but also a soft and welcoming one, the kitchen will set the tone for the whole home.

'The kitchen will set the tone for the whole home.'

The mugs that tell a story

In our grandparents' house when we were growing up, there was a large kitchen dresser, which housed all the crockery and glassware. Our grandfather had screwed hooks into the underside of the shelves, on which hung the family's mugs. Every member of the family had their own mug and whenever someone new joined, a space would be found and another hook would be added, like a crockery tapestry of cousins, uncles and aunts.

We children would use these mugs for everything, from milky tea in the morning to orange squash at teatime and hot chocolate before bed. It was a household that was run around mealtimes and hot beverages, so the one-mug-per-person rule was as much to cut down on the washing up (there was no dishwasher) as it was to honour personal preference.

In this house, nothing matched. The tea tray bore witness to a plethora of tastes: from a Beatrix Potter mug with Mrs Tiggy-Winkle belonging to our mother to a delicate bone china cup with a floral pattern which, you might be surprised to learn, belonged to our grandfather, an outdoorsy man who would mainly be found tinkering on his boat or in the shed.

The house has now passed on to new owners and so many of our memories from that time are viewed through the sepia lens of childhood. We all remember the dresser, with its old cigar box of felt-tip pens and pencils, its plates stacked in great piles on the shelves and of course the mugs, witness to the magical times spent in that house and how lucky we were to have our very own hook.

On colour-coding and other kitchen crimes

We have become a generation obsessed with decanting, labelling, arranging and alphabetising. While there is much satisfaction to be found in a kitchen declutter or a reorganisation of your sock drawer, there is also a fine line between being organised enough to feel in control and, say, arranging your apples by colour. Have we teetered into a dark world of organisational obsession merely for the sake of aesthetics?

TO DECANT OR TO DESIST?

Who knew that pouring things from one container into another, more visually pleasing container would be so satisfying? As well as looking more organised, there are some practical advantages to decanting dried goods into purpose-bought storage containers. Cereals, rice and pasta are likely to last longer in an airtight container than in a half-open packet. They will also be protected from unwelcome visitors, such as pantry moths (shudder). There is also the added benefit of being able to find things more easily and waste less. No one needs four near-empty couscous packets in the back of their cupboard.

There are other times, however, when it really is decanting for decanting's sake. When faced with the question 'Do I need a special container for this?' follow these guidelines:

1. Will the shop-bought packaging keep my food just as fresh?

2. Will decanting this into something else help me to see what it is more clearly?

3. Do I need to go out and buy a new container or do I already have something at home that would work just as well?

4. Am I able to bring my own container to the shop to bypass single-use packaging altogether?

5. Am I doing this purely so that I can take a photo of it afterwards?

6. The following items do not need to be decanted:

Fruit juice and milk: pouring your orange juice into a clear bottle of the exact same size and function as the store-bought carton is pointless.

Yogurt: yogurt containers are designed to keep your yogurt fresh for as long as possible. You do not need to empty them into a new container.

Eggs: moving your eggs from their cardboard container to a plastic container is, again, pointless.

PUT DOWN THE LABEL MAKER

We say this as reformed label-obsessives: put down the label machine. We purchased a label maker that was very exciting as it connected to your phone and you could choose lots of different fonts and icons and colours and it was altogether awesome. But then we got a bit over-enthusiastic and decided to label, well, basically everything. The problem is that the labels didn't come off very easily, so now we are destined to have a load of jars with dog-eared labels that say things like 'mung beans' after that one and only time we bought mung beans. Or they say 'pasta: orecchiette' in a container that has only ever had boring penne in it ever since. Be judicious with your labelling.

ARRANGING ANYTHING BY COLOUR IS A SIGN YOU'VE GONE TO THE DARK SIDE

We have all seen those Pinterest fridges where the shelves are artfully stuffed in a rainbow array of fresh produce: the beetroot nestled next to a bunch of purple grapes that transition seamlessly into tomatoes and strawberries. Kale, lettuce and diced kiwi all hanging out together in green delight. This is not real life and no decent cook would ever arrange their fridge in this way. Likewise, pantries with blue-packaged snacks kept together in little baskets, yellow and orange packets side by side. The same applies to bookshelves.

The best home cooks we know have mismatched spice jars and old jam jars full of obscure homemade condiments. They could probably reach into their cupboards and fridges blindfolded and find what they need immediately, as nothing in their cupboards stays unused and on display for long. There is beauty in utility and nowhere more so than in the kitchen.

Why the British are so good at comfort food

In Britain we get a lot of stick over our cuisine, or lack thereof. Wails of 'But where are the spices?' and, 'Why must everything come with potatoes?' are water off a duck's back to us. Of course, the modern-day reality of British cuisine is one inspired by the hundreds of cultural influences that we are so lucky to have in our country. Food cooked in homes and in restaurants in the UK are now full of flavours from all over the world, from the West Indies to South Asia, and everywhere in between. We are now far more adventurous and open-minded in our cooking than ever before, our cupboards stuffed with gochujang, sumac and dried chipotle peppers, all ingredients that our grandparents might never have tasted.

When we refer to 'traditional British food', however, we think of dishes like shepherd's pie, sausages and mash or a classic roast dinner (see, we did say that potatoes featured heavily). Apart from potatoes, what a lot of these dishes have in common is that they all taste great when eaten in a pub and during cold weather, two things that we happen to have in abundance in Britain.

Traditional British food is really made for cold, wet, grey days when your body is crying out for some carbs and hot gravy. In a country where all the exciting fruit and vegetables are in season for only a small portion of the year, we have had to get creative with pickling and jarring, a trend that is thankfully coming back in vogue. You might not be compelled to order a sticky toffee pudding while sitting on the shores of the Italian Riviera, but that is the point of British food. It's what you want when you come in out of the cold, with mud on your boots, and there's a fire in the grate.

The ultimate chicken pie

On a cold winter's night, there aren't many meals that hit the spot better than a good old-fashioned chicken pie. Making the rough puff pastry is really worth it, for the crispest, most buttery top. Serve with mash and greens, or whatever you fancy.

SERVES 4
COOK TIME: 1 HOUR 20 MINUTES

For the rough puff pastry
250g plain flour
½ tsp salt
180g salted butter, frozen in a block

For the filling
700g chicken thigh fillets
1 tbsp olive oil
20g butter
160g diced pancetta
1 onion, peeled and finely chopped
3 sprigs of thyme, leaves picked
½ bulb of fennel, trimmed and finely chopped
½ leek, halved and cut into 1cm slices
2 tbsp plain flour
100ml dry white wine
400ml chicken stock
100ml double cream
handful of tarragon, roughly chopped
1 egg, beaten
salt and pepper

1. To make the pastry, sift the flour and salt into a mixing bowl. Using a box grater, grate the frozen butter into the bowl. Give it a quick mix to coat each strand of butter in flour, then add 2–3 tablespoons of cold water – just enough to make a rough dough. Tip the dough onto a work surface and briefly knead it to bring it together. Wrap it in cling film and put it in the fridge to chill for 30 minutes.

2. Now make the filling, cut the chicken into 2cm chunks and season with a good pinch of salt. Add the chicken and olive oil to a large sauté pan or wide saucepan over a medium-high heat and fry for about 5 minutes until the chicken is browned all over, but not cooked through. Remove from the pan and set aside.

3. Add the butter to the pan and turn the heat down to low. Add the pancetta and cook for 5 minutes until the fat has rendered out and the pancetta is crisp.

4. Add the onion, thyme leaves and a pinch of salt and cook for about 15 minutes until the onion is soft and just starting to caramelise.

5. Add the fennel and leek to the pan and cook for another 5 minutes until softened.

6. Tip the flour into the pan and beat to form a paste. Cook for 1 minute until it smells biscuity, then pour in the wine and mix well. Gradually pour in the chicken stock, beating all the while until smooth. Bring the mixture to the boil to thicken it. Turn the heat down, then tip in the chicken and simmer for 15 minutes.

7. Add the cream and tarragon to the chicken, then season to taste with salt and pepper. Pour the mixture into an 18cm round pie dish and put it in the fridge to chill.

8. Roll out the pastry in one direction until it is about 25cm long and 0.5cm thick. Fold the top third down, then fold the bottom end up and over the top part. Rotate the pastry 90° clockwise, then roll it out again in one direction until it's 25cm long. Fold the two ends in as before, then put it back in the fridge to chill for 20 minutes.

9. Roll out the pastry to about 3mm thick, then cut out a circle a little bigger than your pie dish. Using the pastry offcuts, cut out a few strips as wide as the pie dish rim.

10. Brush the rim of the pie dish with beaten egg. Press the pastry strips around the rim to cover it completely, then brush this pastry with a little beaten egg. Carefully arrange the pastry circle on top and trim off the excess pastry with a sharp knife. Press the edges on the rim with a fork to seal, then brush the surface with egg. Chill for at least 30 minutes.

11. Heat the oven to 210°C/190°C fan.

12. Pop the pie on a baking tray. Brush again with beaten egg, then bake for 25–30 minutes until the pastry is golden and crisp and the filling is piping hot. Serve it up.

'On a winter's night, there aren't many meals that hit the spot better than a chicken pie.'

Broccoli soup with Stilton croutons

A vibrant green soup is often precisely the thing you need to brighten up a dull winter day. A crunchy sidekick is always welcome, and these Stilton toasts are just the ticket.

SERVES 4
COOK TIME: 35 MINUTES

20g butter
1 onion, peeled and finely chopped
5g thyme, leaves picked
300g Maris Piper potatoes
2 cloves of garlic, finely chopped
1.2 litres chicken or vegetable stock
1 head of broccoli
100g baby leaf spinach
100ml double cream
4 slices of sourdough bread
50g Cheddar, grated
50g Stilton, crumbled
salt and pepper

1. Heat a large saucepan over a medium heat, add the butter, then add the onion and thyme leaves and cook for 15 minutes until the onion has softened and is just starting to caramelise.

2. Peel the potatoes and cut them into 2cm chunks.

3. Add the garlic to the pan and cook for 1 minute, then tip in the potatoes. Pour in the stock and bring it up to a simmer. Once bubbling, cook for 5 minutes.

4. Cut the broccoli (stalks and all) into equal-sized chunks, then add to the pan. Simmer for 10 minutes.

5. Add the spinach and cream, then cook for 1 minute more.

6. Carefully ladle the mixture into a blender, then whizz until smooth. Pour it back into the pan and season to taste with salt and pepper. Keep warm over a low heat.

7. Heat your grill to high. Put the bread on a baking tray and grill for 2 minutes until golden.

8. Mix the two cheeses together. Flip the bread over, add the cheese on top, then return to the grill for 2 minutes until the cheese is melted and bubbly.

9. Spoon the soup into warmed bowls and serve with a piece of toast.

Potatoes: a Piglet ranking

Ask anyone to rank the way they like their potatoes and you will kick off an impassioned and long-lasting debate. If you are looking for a dinner party conversation starter, this is it (although you may never look at some friends the same way again). Here is the official Piglet potato ranking: the ultimate experts in cosy comfort, weighing in on the ultimate comfort food.

TIER A (SPUD HEAVEN)

- Dauphinoise potatoes
- Hash browns
- Jacket potatoes
- Mashed potatoes
- Roast potatoes
- Skinny fries

TIER B (STILL POTATOTALLY DELICIOUS)

- Boiled new potatoes
- Chunky chips
- Curly fries
- Latkes
- Potato wedges
- Rosti
- Sweet potato fries

TIER C (MEH)

- Boiled potatoes
- Chips from the chippy
- Duchess potatoes
- Gnocchi
- Potato salad

So there you have it, the ranking that you never knew you needed. Please feel free to disagree, as is your right as the true potato enthusiast we hope you are.

Creamed corn and tuna jacket potatoes

SERVES 2
COOK TIME: 1 HOUR

2 large baking potatoes
1 tbsp olive oil
20g butter
1 onion, peeled and finely chopped
270g tinned sweetcorn, drained
150ml double cream
150ml vegetable stock
60g Cheddar
30g pickled jalapeños
150g tinned tuna in olive oil, drained
10g chives, finely chopped
salt and pepper

You already know where we stand on the jacket potato. How to make this top-tier potato even better? Add tuna and sweetcorn, but make it extra fantastic. The creamed corn base spiked with spicy jalapeños is a really comforting thing to tuck into on a chilly evening.

1. Heat the oven to 220°C/200°C fan.

2. Stab the potatoes all over with a fork, then pop them on a baking tray. Drizzle them with the olive oil and a good pinch of salt, then rub all over their surface. Bake for 1 hour.

3. Meanwhile, heat a saucepan over a medium heat, add the butter, then add the onion and cook for 15 minutes until softened and just starting to caramelise.

4. Add the sweetcorn to the pan, along with the double cream and stock, then bring it up to a simmer. Cook for 5 minutes.

5. Whizz up about half the mixture with a stick blender, then grate in the Cheddar. Finely chop about two-thirds of the jalapeños and add them to the pan, along with the tuna. Stir to melt the cheese, then season to taste with salt and pepper.

6. Once your potatoes are cooked, halve them and spoon the tuna mixture into the centre. Sprinkle with the remaining jalapeños and chopped chives, then serve.

The Living Room

A room for living in

If the kitchen is the beating heart of the home – functional, dynamic and essential – the living room is the equivalent of a deep exhale. Its raison d'être is to embody a space for relaxation, togetherness and exerting yourself to an absolute minimum. We have many names for this room – living room, drawing room, lounge, sitting room, parlour (okay, relax, no one is calling it that) – but whatever the moniker, the purpose remains the same: to sit down and chill out.

When we were growing up, our sitting room was a space of peaceful (and sometimes not so peaceful) family co-existence. It was home to the only television in the house, so it was also the battleground for endless remote control power-grabs – and not just between the children. We would get home from school and spread our homework out on the carpet, lying on our stomachs with one eye on *Neighbours* or *Home and Away*. There were jumbled bookshelves and an ever-present pile of discarded newspapers next to our dad's armchair. The sofas were faded but comfortable and, in a family of zealous nappers, it would not be uncommon to find someone asleep on them in the middle of the day. Living rooms are for the whole family and as such need a certain amount of versatility. Above all they should be inviting, so that everyone wants to spend time in there, together.

For your living room to reflect the Piglet ethos of living comfortably and joyfully, there are a few areas to consider:

SOFAS AND ARMCHAIRS

We love a deep sofa: one that encourages you to curl your legs up under you and make polite perching difficult (no one should ever be politely perching in your sitting room). Think more Gryffindor common room and less therapist's waiting room. Sofa cushions are a great way to add colour and personality to your living room and can be swapped out if you want a change in look.

THE ELEPHANT IN THE ROOM: THE TELEVISION

If there is one thing that 99 per cent of our living rooms are going to have, it's a television. They aren't the most stylish addition to your room, but they are what they are. And what they are is brilliant. If you worship at the altar of comfort as we do, it would be hard to deny that relaxing in front of the TV isn't a big part of that. You can hide them, if you like, behind clever folding cupboards or pretend they are an ever-changing piece of framed art, or you could just accept them as they are. No one ever walks into a room and thinks, 'I simply cannot believe these people watch telly!'

THINK STORAGE

To make the most of this versatile space without it being a constant mess, try to factor in some storage solutions. If the room doubles as a playroom, is there space for the toys to be cleared away at the end of the day or moved to a dedicated corner of the room? If it doubles as a home office, can the work clutter be put into drawers? Can cosy blankets be popped into a basket, out of the way until you need them?

WEAR, TEAR AND SPILLAGES

In all likelihood, food and drink will be consumed on the premises. Your living room may be your main entertaining space or form part of your dining area, so we need to be practical and realistic about spillages and stains. Rugs, as opposed to wall-to-wall carpet, can be a saving grace when it comes to spillages as they are easier to clean or can be sent out for specialist cleaning if needed. If you have furniture that is vulnerable to water marks, make sure you have lots of coasters scattered around. If investing in new sofas or armchairs, it is worth looking at the durability and ease of cleaning the fabric: is it resistant to high wear and tear; are the covers removable and, ideally, machine washable?

LET THERE BE LIGHT

Lighting should be soft, warm and diffused: table lamps are your friends, as are wall-mounted sconces. You should never, ever need to turn on the overhead light, unless you are carrying out some sort of forensic examination.

A guide to the perfect 'picky bits' plate

If we could eat a selection of little morsels for dinner on the sofa every night, we would. Building the perfect picky bits plate calls for a bit of creativity, along with a formula to keep things balanced. You want a variety of textures, colours and flavours that range from fatty to sharp. Here is a picky bits game plan.

- Something crunchy (x 1): sourdough crackers, crisps, toast

- Something spreadable (x 1–2): hummus, tzatziki, caramelised onion chutney, mango chutney, butter

- Something healthy (x 1–2): sliced apple, celery sticks, cucumber sticks, carrot sticks, chicory leaves, grapes

- Something sharp (x 1–2): pickled onions, olives, cornichons, caperberries, sauerkraut, kimchi, pickled beetroots

- Something fatty (x 2–3): Cheddar, Comté, Gorgonzola, garlic and herb cream cheese, ham, saucisson/salami, sausage rolls, anchovies, 7-minute boiled eggs

THE LIVING ROOM

The nook: creating space for hobbies

There has never been a better time to learn new skills or take up new hobbies. We are overwhelmed with incredible resources to help us discover our next project. You can find tutorials on YouTube on anything from learning how to crochet, to upcycling vintage furniture, to installing your own electrics (maybe don't do this). More and more people are trying to dedicate space in their home for their own passion projects and hobbies.

While we would all love an abundance of airy, light-filled empty rooms in our houses, the reality is usually somewhat different. We have had to get creative, by carving out little dedicated spaces within existing rooms. Enter: the nook.

THE WRAPPING STATION

Is a space dedicated to gift wrapping essential? No. But would it be fabulous? Indeed it would. We say this particularly if you have entered the peak gift-wrapping era of your life, which is when you have a young family. Children's parties come at you hard and fast, it's always somebody's birthday and then bam! it's Christmas. All of a sudden you are that person who buys their gift cards in bulk and stocks up on Christmas wrapping paper in the January sales. Having all your wrapping paper and necessities in one place is such a time-saver. No more hunting for the Sellotape or for an envelope. It could be as simple as keeping a drawer free in the kitchen or having a box you slide out from under the sofa.

THE READING NOOK

All you need is a cosy armchair in the corner of the room, with a good reading light and a bookshelf to house your favourite titles. The key is that you are able to melt away into your book and become more or less invisible to other members of the household; to savour the simple joy of having a quiet space to escape the everyday and disappear into stories of lands from far, far away.

THE SEWING AND KNITTING CORNER

If you are keen on making your own clothes, then having a sewing machine to hand is hugely helpful. A small table set up in the corner of a room for the sewing machine to remain plugged in, threaded and ready to go means that projects can carry over days and be picked up when time allows.

'Savour the simple joy of a quiet space to escape the everyday.'

THE ART AREA

This should be a space that doesn't need to stay too pristine. A few paint splatters here and there are more than likely, and it would be handy to keep all your paints, brushes and cloths in one area. A bright corner of the living room with natural light works well for this purpose, or alternatively garden sheds and greenhouses make it possible to keep the mess outside the house and provide the perfect excuse for a bit of creative time alone with your thoughts.

A GARDENING SPACE

In Daphne du Maurier's *Rebecca*, the great house of Manderley has a cuttings room, solely for the preparation and arranging of flowers; we have been obsessed with this idea ever since reading the book. Keen gardeners are installing greenhouses to create a plant sanctuary: a peaceful place where you can propagate, pot, prune and harvest, surrounded by your plants and the warm smell of compost. Greenhouses are also doubling up as entertaining spaces: add some string lights and some chairs and you have the perfect spot for summer evening cocktails.

The joy of rearranging

It would be a random Saturday afternoon when we would suddenly be gripped by the desire – no, the need – to rearrange our bedrooms. Our parents would hear the ominous sound of furniture scraping over floorboards as we heaved and hauled our beds to the other side of the room. Much parental grumbling and muttering later and the bed would be where the chest of drawers was, which would be where the desk was, which would be where the bed was and ta-da! it's a whole new room.

If you are in a bit of a funk and are fed up with your space, it is something we highly recommend. We tend to get stuck in ruts: furniture placement is often decided on a whim on the day we move into a new place and never changed.

Before buying anything new, look around the house and see what could be rearranged to give your room a fresh look. All too often we buy items not because we need them, but because we want that feeling of 'new'. An armchair from the spare room could be moved to the living room and suddenly it feels new again. If moving furniture feels like too much of an effort, you could try switching up smaller pieces, like table lamps, artwork and rugs.

We could start seeing our home as something less static and more of a movable feast that can change, grow organically and be in constant movement of style. Let's think of it the way we might think of our wardrobes. When we buy a new top we think of all the other items we own that it could go with; we mix it up and wear it many different ways. The same can apply to the items in our home. Small changes make a big difference: by updating framed photos, changing lampshades and moving ornaments, we can breathe life into old things and fall in love with them again.

Welcoming the outside in

The Germans have a term for opening the windows and letting fresh air in: *luften*. It is so important in Germany that some landlords stipulate it in their tenancy agreements. Opening all the windows and 'changing the air' of the house has many practical benefits, such as avoiding the build-up of moisture, as well as being beneficial to our physical and mental wellbeing.

After a nasty family bout of norovirus, a doctor advised us to open all the windows and doors for 10 minutes a day to let fresh air run through the house and allow germs to dissipate. This is something we now do regularly, even in the depths of winter, and the whole household feels better for it. Everyone in the house slightly under the weather? *Luften*. Cabin fever after spending Christmas in a house full of people? *Luften*. The vibes simply feeling off? *Luften*.

Fresh air is just one of the elements that improve our mood. Natural light, birdsong and the physical movement associated with being outside are beneficial to our overall wellbeing. Green spaces have a proven positive effect on our mental health and may help us to feel calmer and more grounded. Regularly exposing yourself to natural light as soon as possible when you wake up can improve sleep quality (although in the winter months you might already have been up for a while before any natural light appears).

Here are some ways we can incorporate the beneficial elements of the outdoors into our interior design choices.

MAKE THE MOST OF ANY NATURAL LIGHT

Get as much daylight as possible into the room. If you have the luxury of large windows, try not to restrict the light with heavy shutters. For privacy or to keep the heat out, sheer curtains or blinds in a natural fabric work beautifully.

USE NATURAL MATERIALS

Wood is such a warming material. It never feels overly cold to the touch, has a beautiful texture and will absorb all the scuffs and stains of everyday life with dignity. Don't be afraid to mix different types of wood in a room. Woods with neutral undertones, such as walnut or white oak, are extremely versatile and pair well with woods with warm or cooler undertones. Consider the grain patterns: woods with pronounced grain, such as oak or ash, add visual interest, whereas fine-grained woods, such as maple or cherry, can provide a more modern, sleek look while retaining that natural warmth.

Natural stone will age wonderfully, gaining a patina over the years that adds character to any house. When considering textiles, it will come as no surprise that we would always opt for natural fibres. Linen, wool, jute and cotton are hardwearing, versatile and appropriate throughout the home, from cushion covers to rugs, from curtains to bed linen.

INCORPORATE GREENERY

You don't need a lot of space to add a few houseplants to a room for an instant botanical feel. Some plants are mercifully forgiving of neglect and will happily sit on a shelf, looking green and lush, with minimal attention. Peace lilies, snake plants and epipremnums are our go-to for hardy houseplants that provide a lot of greenery and won't hold a grudge if you forget to water them. Others can be more fickle, until you perfect the balance of light, temperature and moisture. You do become rather attached to your houseplants though, especially the more sensitive ones, so be warned.

CHOOSE A COLOUR PALETTE INSPIRED BY THE OUTDOORS

This doesn't have to mean painting everything in your house green. Rather, think about how colours complement each other in nature. Earthy tones create an inviting and grounded atmosphere by evoking the natural colours of the outdoors. Warm shades like ochre and earthy reds work nicely with cooler tones like sage green or muted blue. When opting for neutrals, consider off-whites like stone or sand to avoid any stark contrast with your natural colours.

APPRECIATE NATURE IN ALL ITS FORMS

Incorporating natural elements into your home is more than a design choice, it is a way to bring balance and beauty into your everyday life. By inviting sunlight, greenery and organic textures into your space, you can create an environment that is both tranquil and inspiring. From the textured warmth of wood to nature-inspired colours, every element can help you feel more in tune with the world. Start with a pot of supermarket basil on the windowsill (see page 142) and see where it takes you.

'Green spaces may help us to feel calmer and more grounded.'

How to collect and display art in your home

Displaying art on your walls or surfaces is a great way to put your own stamp on your home and add interest, colour and personality. Knowing what to buy, how much to spend and where to buy it, however, can be daunting. The art world is cloaked in a veil of mystique that can make you feel out of the loop and unsure of where to start. Price points vary wildly, and bespoke framing can cost more than the artwork itself.

At Piglet, we believe that leaning into what you love will always trump doing things 'the right way' and the same applies to your art collection. Overleaf are a few ideas on how to get started.

DISCOVER YOUR STYLE

It is worth investing some time into discovering what it is that you like before you commit to any purchase. Be open-minded, stroll around art fairs, take a look around local galleries when on holiday and keep an eye out for interesting items at flea markets. Social media is a great way to browse art from the comfort of your screen, by following individual artists or galleries. Soon enough your eye will start to pick out themes or styles that you are drawn to again and again.

START SMALL AND AFFORDABLE

You don't need to spend big bucks to build up a collection. Measure value in terms of your own enjoyment of a piece. This will open up a whole world of art that you might not have been aware of. Secondhand pieces are a great way to buy affordable art and often come already framed, which keeps costs down.

SUPPORT LOCAL AND YOUNG ARTISTS

Art colleges will have galleries and end-of-year exhibitions where you can meet new artists and buy their work. It is often far more affordable than buying from established artists and you will be encouraging young talent.

If you follow an artist you love online, get in touch with them and ask them about specific pieces, pricing and any upcoming shows. Usually they will be happy to engage with someone enthusiastic about their work and you will be building a rapport that can give even more meaning to the pieces you like.

MIX AND MATCH STYLES

If you have a broad interest in art, then vary your pieces. Mixing media and styles makes for an interesting and diverse collection. Likewise with sizes and frames – try to avoid too much uniformity.

'Measure value in terms of your own enjoyment of a piece of art.'

FRAMING AND HANGING

Choosing the right frame for your artwork can be tricky. If you're not sure, it may be worth taking advice from your local framer, who can help you choose the size of the frame and the mount. A small painting might benefit from a wide mount to draw the eye to the heart of the artwork, for example. Classical pieces don't always need heavy or ornate frames, so be open-minded about the style you choose. Sometimes you won't know what is right until you get that aha! moment.

Keep an eye out for frames you like in vintage shops – we have found some beautiful frames in charity shops. Learn how to hang the art on the wall properly, to ensure it stays in place. There are great tutorials on YouTube that can help with this.

COLLECTING TAKES TIME; BUY ONLY WHAT YOU LOVE

Don't go into this chasing the 'next big thing' and looking to build value. These are items that you will be looking at every day, so make sure they appeal to you. Buy what you love and you will end up with a varied collection of art with a story about how you found each piece.

THE LIVING ROOM

The Bathroom

Making a splash in the bathroom

The bathroom is often an afterthought when it comes to how we want our house to look and, more importantly, feel. At Piglet, we think any space in your house, no matter how small or how functional, is an opportunity to showcase your personality and create a space that brings you joy. Bathrooms – especially if installed by a previous inhabitant – can be devoid of colour and soul, and can be expensive and time-consuming to change. Often, they are blank canvases of white tile and porcelain, intended to please everyone and therefore pleasing no one.

The wonderful thing about being a Piglet-y person is that you can make any space your own, no matter how uninspiring the canvas. The bathroom is just as deserving of this treatment as the rest of your home. You don't need an indoor spa complete with palm-frond-wafting aides to create a place of relaxation.

'We think any space in your house is an opportunity to showcase your personality.'

BE INSPIRED BY SOMETHING YOU ALREADY HAVE AND LOVE

When looking for inspiration on how to uplift a space, we find it helpful to start with something small. You might have, for example, a small ceramic pot that you love and want to place in the bathroom. It is entirely reasonable to make this the basis of your colour palette. Pick out the shades in the pot that you like and incorporate them throughout the room – for the wall colour or tiles, or in a lampshade or soap dish. In doing this, we create intentionality in our design and give cohesion to the space, without everything looking overly matchy-matchy.

COLOUR IS YOUR BEST FRIEND

The most impactful way to uplift a room is to paint it. Even if your bathroom is small, it is likely to have some non-tiled walls that you can throw some colour at. You will be amazed at the difference a coat of paint can make. Dark and moody colours, for example, can work wonderfully in small spaces, especially with pops of brighter colour elsewhere in the room.

THINK ABOUT TEXTILES

In the bathroom, textiles are in abundance. Good-quality towels and bath mats add softness and make the room feel welcoming. A blind over a window will make the space feel more like a room you want to spend time in. Add a linen shower curtain to hide the plastic one underneath. Be bold with colour and patterns and enjoy the interchangeability of these bathroom essentials.

FORGET ABOUT PERFECTION

Your collection of mismatched bottles of shampoo, conditioners and cleansers can stay exactly where they are. You don't need uniformity or perfectly lined-up containers. No one is going to walk into your bathroom and be horrified that you cracked open a new shower gel before the last one was finished. If you love the sight of all your products beautifully organised, then go for it! But if that's not your way, don't worry.

BITS AND BOBS

Your bathroom can be spruced up with the addition of all sorts of little things, from posy vases, to candles, to framed artwork on the wall. Just make sure they can withstand the humidity of a long steamy bath.

How to be useless to everyone: take a long bath

Ah, the simple indulgence that is taking a long bath. Not only are baths said to reduce stress, alleviate joint and muscle ache and improve circulation, but they have the wonderful advantage of providing a blissful slice of time just for yourself. Getting clean is a happy by-product of having a bath but is certainly not the intended purpose. You might emerge smelling nicer than when you went in but no, the bath is for wallowing.

The best thing about taking a bath is that you can't be of service to anyone once you're in. You can't hunt down someone's lost socks when you're in the bath. You can't answer the door, you can't make a start on dinner and you certainly can't reply to an email. If anyone shouts a question through the door, just lower your ears under the water – it works a treat. And don't forget to lock the door.

'Baths have the wonderful advantage of providing a blissful slice of time just for yourself.'

FIRST THINGS FIRST: SET THE SCENE

There is nothing worse than lowering your body into hot, heavenly smelling water only to realise two minutes later that you've forgotten something essential, or that your towel is out of reach. Always remember the following:

- Alert the household to the fact that you are having a bath and this means *Do not disturb*.

- Ensure there is enough hot water for the bath. The sinking feeling of lukewarm water coming out of the tap and the knowledge that your bath won't be quite hot enough is sub-optimal.

- Light a candle. Even better, light two. They smell nice and bring a sense of ceremony to the occasion.

- Have two towels on hand. A small one that you can use to dry your hands if you want to reach for something and a large one to wrap yourself in after the bath.

- Make sure your hair is up and out of your face.

CHOOSE YOUR POTIONS

If you love **bubbles** in your bath, then consider putting the bubble bath in before any oils, which weigh down the bubbles, causing them to melt away quickly.

We love **bath oils**: they are gentle on the skin and there are essential oils to suit every mood. You only need a small amount and the bathroom is instantly transformed into an incredible-smelling steam room.

Bath salts, such as Epsom salts help relieve muscle soreness and tension and can calm your nervous system by replenishing magnesium levels in the body.

A long bath is an excellent opportunity for a **face mask**. The heat of the water opens up your facial pores, boosting the benefits of your face mask.

Have a **loofah** or a mitt on hand to give everything a scrub before getting out.

'Candles bring a sense of ceremony to bathtime.'

TAKE SOME ENTERTAINMENT

Many people love a long bath for the chance to enjoy their own thoughts and think through problems. However, if you have no desire to spend too long in your own head, then don't forget to take a book or magazine into the bath with you, or set up your iPhone, tablet or smart speaker with a favourite podcast or mood-enhancing playlist – just keep it away from the water.

SNACKS ARE OPTIONAL

Now this is divisive … We believe that eating in the bath is simply honouring your right as an adult to do whatever you like. There is an argument that getting biscuit crumbs in your bath is counter-productive, but we say it just adds some seasoning.

CHOOSE YOUR TIME OF DAY

The obvious time for a bath is the evening: it's relaxing, and the timing ensures a seamless transition from bath to bed. Another advantage is that you could enjoy a glass of wine at the same time, which cannot be understated.

Baths in the morning feel even more indulgent somehow. These are for those rare but wonderful duvet days when you can get out of the bath and straight onto the sofa.

'Baths in the morning feel even more indulgent somehow.'

The humblebrag that is the downstairs loo

The British horror of 'showing off' means that pasting evidence of our personal accolades and achievements all over the house is rarely done. You are unlikely to find framed certificates of degrees in the sitting room or sporting trophies on shelves. So where do you display that photo of you shaking hands with Obama? Not to worry, we have a solution: the downstairs cloakroom.

The downstairs loo is a place free of judgement. It has neutral status. It is a room that can shout 'Look what I've achieved! Look who I've met! Look where I've been!' without the repercussions of being unfriended immediately. What might be considered gauche and over-the-top in the rest of the house becomes suddenly self-deprecating when displayed in the downstairs loo. 'Oh, you noticed the newspaper clipping of that time I rescued a dog from a freezing lake, did you? It was nothing really, anyone would have done the same.' Kate Winslet famously kept her Oscar in her downstairs loo, so that her guests could privately rehearse their imaginary acceptance speeches in front of the mirror.

As for decor, the cloakroom is a freestanding entity: it need not have any design affiliation with the rest of the house. It is a place to have some fun with your creativity and give your guests something to look at when they are in there. Wallpapering is a popular choice, as this room tends to be small and won't require reams and reams of expensive paper. A little shelf for books or poetry is a nice touch, again giving a chance to show your guests who you are.

DOWNSTAIRS CLOAKROOM ESSENTIALS FOR WHEN YOU HAVE GUESTS:

- Fresh hand towels

- Hand soap and hand moisturiser

- Spare loo rolls: we like to have these in an obvious place to avoid any panicky moments

- A candle, flowers or reed diffuser is always a welcome addition

Beyond the practical essentials, the room is your own little space for anything silly or that you are proud of but don't want to shout about from the rooftops.

'The cloakroom is a place to have some fun with your creativity.'

The Garden

Growing things: why does it make us so happy?

It is wonderful to us that you can buy a little packet of seeds and watch them transform into something that you can eat, smell or simply look at in delight. It is pure magic. When it works, that is. The bit in between planting the seed and the end result is where the difficulty lies. Too much water, not enough water, an early frost, a late frost, not pruned enough, pruned at the wrong time, an uncommonly humid summer, a garden aphid invasion. Sigh. But then, by some miracle, you get it right and you pluck your first cherry tomato, warmed by the sun, and pop it into your mouth. Its flavour bursts on your tongue and it tastes like the most perfect tomato you have ever eaten and of something else: the sweet, sweet taste of a job well done.

SO WHY DOES GARDENING CHEER US UP SO MUCH?

At Piglet we love it when things slow down enough to really enjoy them. The most surprising discovery when we started gardening was that the literal fruits of our labours were not the biggest prize. Instead, it was the many small moments of pleasure along the way: the satisfaction of an afternoon spent in the garden potting up bulbs or the day you spot the first shoot poking out of the soil.

Planting and growing things is an easy and accessible way to connect with nature while feeling like you are doing something productive. The bugs you come across in the soil, the smell of fresh compost, the background sounds of the birds as you work, all contribute to regulating the nervous system and calming the noise in our minds.

Gardening is an activity that combines creativity with problem-solving. What plants will look good in my garden/on my balcony/on my windowsill and how can I achieve my vision? How can I make the most of the space that I have? What can I make with the food that I grow? It requires thought, time and consideration.

Lastly, any time that our hands are buried in soil is time when they are not holding a phone, which we can all agree is a good thing.

'Gardening is an easy way to connect with nature while feeling like you are doing something productive.'

The lost art of picnicking

Eating outdoors makes everything taste delicious. Even a slightly soggy sandwich and a bag of crisps will taste better on a park bench with the sun on your face than it will when eaten sitting at your desk. But you can also do better than that. So much of the pleasure in picnicking is in the anticipation: wrapping up parcels of deliciousness to be enjoyed later under wide open skies, without the glow of a phone in sight.

THE INGREDIENTS FOR THE PERFECT PICNIC

A big soft **blanket** is key. Don't be stingy on size so that you don't have to ration blanket real-estate to one butt cheek each. A couple of overlapping blankets works just as well.

Think through what **tableware** (blanket-ware?) you will need. A full set of crockery plates looks lovely but weighs a tonne, so if you *are* venturing to a location far from the car, you might want to consider something more lightweight. Glassware, on the other hand, is sometimes worth the effort of hefting around. Chilled rosé tastes far crisper from a wine glass than when served in a plastic cup.

Great company is an essential element to any picnic, even if that company is just yourself.

OUR FAVOURITE PICNIC FOOD

Picnics are all about sharing: sharing a favourite spot, sharing room on the blanket and, of course, sharing food. These are some of our essentials for a great picnic:

Homemade dips: easily transportable and great to snack on while you get everything else laid out (see page 139 for our absolute favourite dip to take on a picnic). Pair with a jumbo bag of crisps or pre-prepared crudités.

Something pastry-based: whether it's a quiche, a savoury tart or some sausage rolls, pastry is the perfect vehicle for picnic food and tastes delicious cold. Slice the tart beforehand or, for that extra wow factor, present it whole and cut it up in situ.

Fruit: you can never go wrong with a big bowl of sliced strawberries sprinkled with fresh mint. For hot days we love to slice watermelon into triangular pieces, which can be handed round easily and are the perfect refreshing fruit to eat in the sunshine.

A sweet treat to end on: a tin of homemade cookies, saved strategically until the end and presented with a flask of coffee will be just what everyone needs to fuel them for the walk home.

OUR TOP PICNICS

The picnic with a view: the ascent may be steep and you might question why you decided to lug a hefty picnic all the way up a hill, but the payoff is always worth it. Your legs might be burning, but there is nothing quite like the feeling of flopping down onto the ground and biting into a well-deserved sandwich, with a wide and beautiful view to look at.

The beach picnic: we admit that these are fickle in nature. We have all had beach picnics blighted by wind, rain or rising tides. But when they *do* go well, they really are superior. Coming back to the beach after a swim in the sea, you sit on a towel warmed by the sun and you get handed something delicious to eat as you blink salty sea water from your eyes.

The park picnic: highly accessible, the park picnic is low buy-in and high reward. Perfect for a spontaneous sunny Saturday with friends, this often goes on until sunset.

The event picnic: in the UK, we love a summer event that involves a good picnic. Open-air theatre, concerts and opera are all staples of the British summer season, and bringing your own picnic really adds to the occasion.

The mini-picnic: this occurs any time you take your food outside with the sole intention of enjoying it in the fresh air. A sandwich and an orange on a park bench during your lunch break or a cup of coffee and croissant perched on a sunny garden wall can be counted as mini-picnics, their enjoyment distilled and fortified by their simplicity.

TIPS AND TRICKS

- Stay away from food that will get sweaty in a picnic cooler, such as soft cheeses or delicate salad leaves.

- Sliced tomatoes can make sandwiches soggy. If you are partial to a tomato in a sandwich, placing it strategically between lettuce leaves may prevent sogginess. Alternatively, take your tomatoes in a separate container.

- If you want to travel light, opt for food that comes in its own natural packaging. Hard-boiled eggs, for example, transport well and can be meditatively peeled and enjoyed with a twist of salt. Whole apples leave nearly nothing behind.

- Always take a small bag for your rubbish. That way, you can keep any mess contained, ready for the first bin you find.

'At Piglet we love it when things slow down enough to really enjoy them.'

Spinach and feta rolls

SERVES 4
COOK TIME: 40 MINUTES

400g frozen whole leaf spinach
2 tbsp olive oil
1 red onion, peeled and finely diced
1 clove of garlic
1 tsp fennel seeds
1 tsp chilli flakes
20g parsley, finely chopped
200g feta
grated zest of 1 lemon
320g ready-rolled puff pastry
1 egg, beaten
20g sesame seeds
salt and pepper

A picnic is incomplete without a sausage roll or veggie equivalent, and these are real crowd pleasers. You can freeze them uncooked for up to 3 months, then cook them straight from frozen.

1. Put the frozen spinach into a large bowl and cover with warm water. Leave to sit and defrost for a bit.

2. Put a small frying pan over a medium heat and pour in the olive oil. Add the onion and cook for 20 minutes until soft and caramelised. Grate in the garlic and cook for another minute, then tip it into a large mixing bowl to cool down.

3. Toast the fennel seeds in a small saucepan over a medium heat for 1 minute, then tip them into a pestle and mortar along with the chilli flakes, and bash them to a coarse powder. Tip these in with the onion.

4. Run warm water over the spinach to thaw out any last bits of ice, then drain it in a colander. Taking the spinach in chunks, squeeze out any moisture with your hands, then roughly chop it.

5. Add the spinach and parsley to the onion bowl, then crumble in the feta. Add the lemon zest and give everything a good mix. Season to taste with salt and pepper.

6. Unroll the puff pastry and spoon the spinach mixture in a line the length of the long side of the pastry, about one-third of the way in. Brush the pastry edges with beaten egg, then fold the long side over the filling to meet the opposite edge. Press the edges down to seal them, then trim off any excess pastry and press the edges with a fork to seal neatly.

7. Brush the beaten egg all over the pastry. Sprinkle the tops with sesame seeds. Place on a tray and chill in the fridge for 20 minutes.

8. Heat the oven to 220°C/200°C fan. Line a baking tray with baking parchment.

9. Cut the roll into four equal pieces and arrange on the lined baking tray. Bake for 15–20 minutes, or until the pastry is golden and crisp. Eat them hot or cold.

THE GARDEN

Smoked aubergine dip

A good dip never goes amiss at a picnic. This one combines smoky aubergine, spicy harissa and a touch of tahini for creaminess. It's perfect for dunking your crudités, crisps or chunks of baguette into.

SERVES 4
COOK TIME: 10 MINUTES

1 aubergine
1 small clove of garlic
1 tbsp smoked harissa paste
2 tbsp pomegranate molasses
2 tbsp tahini
juice of ½ lemon
20g pomegranate seeds
a few flat-leaf parsley leaves
salt

1. If you have a gas hob, put the aubergine directly over a medium flame and cook for about 10 minutes, rotating it regularly so that it cooks evenly. Alternatively, you could whack the aubergine under a very hot grill, or on a barbecue. You want the skin to get very charred and wrinkly, and the flesh to be soft. Leave on a plate to cool slightly.

2. When the aubergine is cool enough to handle, rub off the skin and cut off the green stem. Shred the flesh with a fork, then add to a bowl.

3. Grate in the garlic and spoon in the harissa paste, pomegranate molasses and tahini, along with the lemon juice. Give everything a good mix, then season to taste with salt.

4. Spoon into a lidded container and top with pomegranate seeds and some roughly chopped parsley. Serve with lots of things to dip in there.

How to make the most of supermarket herbs

In the supermarket, your hand wavers between the packet of pre-cut basil and the potted basil. A voice whispers in your head: 'This time will be different … this time, you will keep the basil alive …' At home, you place the pot of basil on the windowsill, filled with determination. Oh, the pesto you'll make! Two weeks later the remains of a wilted basil plant land with a resounding thunk at the bottom of the bin. Packet basil it is then, at least until the little voice in your head comes back: 'This time will be different …'

If this sounds familiar, read on for our top tips on how to make the most out of herbs that you can easily find in the supermarket.

HOW TO KEEP A POTTED BASIL ALIVE

Basil is a demanding creature. We have contributed to more basil plant deaths than we care to think about, but of all the methods we have tried, this is the one that is the most likely to guarantee success. Note that basil loves warm, sunny spots and hates the cold, so growing it is far more likely to be successful in the summer months!

Repot your supermarket basil into a roomier, terracotta (if possible) pot with some potting soil. The pot needs good drainage holes as it will get all of its water from the bottom only.

Give it a healthy watering to bed it into the soil.

Place the pot in a large bowl or saucer. This is very important as you will only ever water it from the bottom from now on. The saucer needs to be able to hold a good amount of water for the plant to draw on. Place it in a bright, sunshiny spot in your kitchen.

As soon as you see the saucer is dry, top it up again. Basil is a very thirsty plant.

Let the basil settle in for about a week to ten days before you start to harvest any leaves.

When you use leaves from the plant, make sure you cut just above existing leaves to encourage regrowth.

Regularly pinch off the top leaves to encourage bushy regrowth. Remove any flowers to allow the plant to focus its energy on flavour and foliage production.

HOW TO TURN PREPACKED SUPERMARKET MINT INTO YOUR VERY OWN PLANT

Propagating mint is a great way of turning supermarket mint sprigs into a crop that will keep you in mojitos all summer long. Here's how to do it:

Take your mint sprigs and remove most of the leaves from the stem, leaving only those on the top quarter.

Place the stems in jam jars or cups of water on a sunny windowsill.

Keep the water fresh and topped up until the stems start to produce roots – this should happen within a week or two.

Once you have roots, transfer the sprigs to some pots of soil. Keep them watered in a sunny spot and soon you should spot the first new shoots starting to sprout.

Mint spreads rapidly, so avoid planting straight into the ground, as it will quickly take over the whole garden, so opt for pots instead.

HOW TO STORE LEFTOVER SUPERMARKET HERBS

So often we will buy a packet of herbs for a specific recipe, use half the packet and shove the rest into the fridge, only to find the remains weeks later languishing, soggy and limp, in the bottom of the vegetable drawer. Here are some simple ways to avoid waste and have herbs on hand when you don't have time to pop to the shops.

Spread the stems on a baking sheet and freeze them whole. Once frozen, transfer to freezer bags. This works well with woodier herbs such as sage, bay and rosemary as they won't discolour too much and can be added to dishes from frozen.

For more delicate herbs such as parsley, coriander and dill, chop them finely, then add them to ice-cube trays, top up with olive oil, water or stock, then freeze. Once frozen, decant the cubes into freezer bags and add to soups, stews and sauces as needed.

Air drying works best for sturdy herbs such as bay, rosemary, thyme and oregano. Gather small bunches of herbs together and hang them upside down in a warm, dry spot. Give them about one to two weeks to dry, then strip the leaves from the stems and store them in airtight containers in the pantry.

THE GARDEN

Hosting

Hosting, but make it chill

You want to have people round for dinner but are put off because you feel that your place just isn't 'dinner party worthy'. You don't have a matching set of brightly coloured Le Creuset baking dishes, you don't have more than three of the same wine glasses and actually, now that you come to think of it, you don't even have enough chairs. As with so many things, hosting is on a spectrum, with Martha Stewart at one end and 'sitting on the floor eating takeaway pizza' on the other. You will find that great times can be had across the entire spectrum, so if you are less Martha Stewart and more Bridget Jones, fear not. Bridget's most successful dinner party involved blue soup and an omelette, and she remains an inspiration to us all.

To host a successful evening full of warmth, friendship and laughter, you don't need perfection. You don't even need culinary expertise or equipment. All you need is to convey the sense that your guests are treating *you* just with their very presence. It's so nice to make a fuss of your friends! Guests look to the host for guidance on the vibe: a host stressed out by the cooking or the timing or appearances puts everyone slightly on edge. Your guests will want to spend time with you, not be treated like royalty while you rush about with your head in the oven or sweating over a chopping board.

If you want to host a relaxed, warm and fun-filled evening, the following ideas have proven helpful to us in the past:

AMBIENCE IS EVERYTHING

Lighting and music will set the tone for the evening. Candlelight covers a multitude of sins so, if you can, dim the lights and light some candles before anyone arrives, to create a cosy atmosphere as soon as people walk in. Overhead lights are instant mood-killers, so stay away from the switch. Likewise with the music: make sure music is playing before your guests arrive so they settle in quickly; be prepared to switch it up depending on the mood of the party throughout the night.

EVERYONE NEEDS A DRINK IN THEIR HAND ASAP

Having a drink in your hand helps everyone to relax and gives the evening a sense of beginning. We love making a batch of a house cocktail or mocktail ahead of time, which can be easily served out as guests arrive. This is a task that can be delegated to someone else – some guests love to be given a little job to do, especially if they don't know many people there. We like to keep a few of these in reserve (slicing lemons, pouring out some more crisps) for anyone who might be feeling a bit shy or wants to feel useful.

WHEN YOU SERVE THE FOOD IS MORE IMPORTANT THAN WHAT YOU SERVE

Whether you are serving supermarket pizzas or homemade beef Wellington, the key is always the timing. Too early and people will feel rushed and won't have had time to settle in, too late and everyone will be drunk and/or hangry. It's always a good idea to have some pre-dinner snacks available for anyone who arrives 'starving'. If you are serving dinner, aim to have it on the table about an hour after the last guest has arrived, or you might have people leaving before the end of the meal, needing to relieve the babysitter.

ONLY INVITE PEOPLE YOU ACTUALLY LIKE

This sounds obvious but it really isn't. How many times have we invited people over because we feel that we should, or because deep down we want to impress them? People who are going to judge you on the quality of your canapés may not be the people you want to surround yourself with. Admitting anyone into your home shows kindness, generosity and vulnerability: after all, this is where you *live*, where you are free to be yourself. Make sure that the people you allow into it are deserving of the honour.

YOUR PARTY CAN BE BEAUTIFUL WITHOUT BEING FORMAL

Colourful napkins, little bunches of flowers, mismatched crockery: anything that feels authentically *you* will radiate warmth and put everyone at ease. Big sharing plates of food in the centre of the table not only look really inviting but will also encourage everyone to get stuck in and help themselves and each other. You want to build up a mini community around your dining table, through food and conversation.

Seating plans have a reputation for being overly formal, but they needn't be. On the contrary, it removes the awkward milling around as people wait to be seated, and a thoughtful table placement will ensure that each guest gets the most out of their neighbour. If place cards are too formal, scribble a plan in advance on a Post-it so you can seat people verbally instead.

How to create a great tablescape

Tablescaping is one of our favourite ways to get creative when hosting, as it provides an instant wow factor and easily elevates any meal you are serving. If the cooking is the main picture, think of the table as the frame. Here is our approach to setting a stylish table:

1. CHOOSE YOUR THEME OR COLOUR SCHEME

Decide on a **theme** or base **colour** for your tablescape. This could be seasonal (spring florals may not be groundbreaking, but they are certainly pretty), occasion-based (like Christmas or Easter) or based on an aesthetic (for example cottage-core or moody).

We love to take inspiration from one small thing and develop the theme. For example, if someone just gifted you a pair of bright pink tapered candles, they could be the base for your entire scheme, with hints of the same colour in your flowers or table linens.

2. LAYER THE BASE

The first layer to your tablescape will usually be fabric; this will soften the starkness of a bare table and create the base of the look. Don't be afraid to mix colours and patterns, just as you would with your bed linen or cushions on your sofa.

Tablecloths: the easiest way to immediately turn a dinner into an 'occasion' is to throw a cloth over the table. It is so simple yet so impactful. Now in general we aren't huge advocates of ironing, well, anything, but if there were to be one exception it would be for tablecloths. Crumpled tablecloths not only detract from the overall effect but are also impractical – nothing will sit right and glasses will wobble over on the creases. Take the time to iron your tablecloth flat before placing it on the table.

Table runners: table runners are long, slim strips of fabric that run down the centre length of the table; they add structure and depth. They can be placed directly onto the table, for a pop of colour and interest, or layered on top of a tablecloth for added texture.

Napkins: realistically, not many of us will use linen napkins in our day-to-day living (the laundry mountain is big enough as it is), but for special occasions they add such an understated touch of care and attention. Besides, if you have already added a tablecloth, putting the napkins into the same laundry load won't make much of a difference.

'To host a successful event full of warmth, friendship and laughter, you don't need perfection.'

Remember, you don't necessarily need your napkins to match your tablecloth, or indeed to match each other. If your tablescape is centred around, for example, the colour green, you could give some of your guests napkins in a green gingham, others plain white with a green trim, or a green leafy pattern. They all work together under the same theme.

Place mats and plate chargers: place mats and plate chargers (which are large, circular 'pretend' plates that you place your real plates on top of) are useful for creating individual place settings and are yet another way to add colour and texture. Mats and chargers work well on bare tables without a tablecloth or runner – beware of overloading the table with too much before you've really started.

3. ADD THE FUNCTIONAL STUFF

Crockery and cutlery: unless you are a professional table stylist, you are unlikely to have multiple sets of crockery or cutlery to go with every theme. Dinnerware is expensive and takes a lot of space to store, so don't worry about not having the ideal plates to match your napkins. Invest in tableware that you love and that you will use again and again in day-to-day life, as well as for guests.

When setting the table, consider whether you want the plates already on the table or whether you will dish up in the kitchen first. Don't stress if you don't have enough knives and forks for every course, just remember to ask your guests to keep them for the next course.

Glassware: make sure there is enough space for everyone to have a water glass and (if serving) a wine glass, and remember to place a jug of water on the table in advance.

4. ADD THE FUN STUFF

Organic decor: adding a natural element to the table will immediately make it welcoming. Flowers don't need to be expensive. One small bunch of supermarket flowers can be split up and trimmed down and added to posy vases all the way down the table. You could add greenery from the garden or your local park. If you don't want to use flowers, use foraged items such as sprigs of leaves, conifers or berries. Whole fruit such as lemons or pomegranates can add aesthetic interest too, depending on your theme.

Candles: from long tapered candles to little tea lights, you can't really go wrong with candles. As well as making everything cosy and atmospheric, candlelight has the added bonus of making everybody look at least 10 per cent more attractive.

Place cards: if you are doing a seating plan, place cards are not only useful in allowing your guests to know where to sit without direction from you, but serve as a helpful reminder to someone who might have forgotten the name of the person they are sitting next to.

'A cosy table is a fun table.'

OUR TOP TIPS FOR TABLESCAPING

- Where possible, re-use what you already have. You don't need to go out and buy a whole load of disposable stuff to fit your theme. Avoid themes that are one-and-done, like 'New Year's Eve 2024' or plastic Halloween pumpkins that you don't have space to store, so they end up in landfill.

- Don't feel you have to tick every box on the tablescape plan: it is fine to build up a collection over the years. Start with versatile pieces, like a neutral tablecloth that goes with everything, and then add to that. Napkins and tablecloths last a lifetime (and longer), so buy good-quality, natural fabrics that will wash well.

- Keep your eyes open in charity shops and thrift stores: you will be amazed how many beautiful things you can find for your table, from vintage tablecloths to little posy vases.

- Don't overload your table so that there is no space left for the main event: the food! You can always move some of the centrepieces, such as flowers and candles, to the side when the food is served, or alternatively keep the serving dishes off the table after everyone has taken what they want.

- Vary the height of your centrepiece to make it more appealing to the eye. If you have tall tapered candles, choose flowers closer to the table, for example. If you have tall stemmed wine glasses, have lowball water glasses.

- It is better for people to be squeezed together than to be too far apart (so don't extend the table unless you have to). A cosy table is a fun table.

- If, at the end of the night, you are left with a table covered in wax drippings, wine stains and crumbs, consider it a success.

Table napkins: three ways

Here are three easy ways to present your napkins that will add a fun detail to your tablescape. It will show that you've taken some time over it, but that you haven't turned into the type of person that spends their day learning how to origami napkins into elaborate woodland creatures.

THE KNOT

This is the simplest one of all, it takes two seconds and you need no other embellishments. Take your napkin by the opposite corners and tie a loose, simple knot in the middle. This looks fun and is easy for your guests to undo before placing on their lap.

THE TIE

Fold your napkin into a rectangle. Tie some string or a piece of ribbon loosely around the napkin, leaving a crease down the centre. Decorate the crease with a sprig of greenery (herbs such as rosemary work well), berries or flowers.

THE BOW

Fold your napkin across the diagonal, then fold the wide edge of the triangle over like you would when making a bandana, until you have one long strip of fabric. Fold each end inwards and downwards to about 45 degrees a third of the way along the strip. Pinch all the fabric together in the middle and feed your napkin ring through the lot – you should end up with a pretty bow to place in the middle of your table setting.

How to make Christmas worth the effort

We are not sure when exactly it happens, but at some point in life, Christmas starts to become more of a chore than the magical gifting and food bonanza that it used to be when we were children. As you leave childhood the reality dawns: that the festive food on the table was thought of, bought by and prepared by someone, and that the presents under the tree are a result of list-making, money-saving and late-night wrapping. It turns out that creating magical memories for others takes a whole lot of effort.

So why do we continue to take on the annual assault course of planning, list-ticking and family drama?

One answer could be that there is little choice, especially if your own children are involved. Some people do opt out of the faff of Christmas, by going away somewhere hot where they can avoid everyone until it's all over. This always seems most appealing sometime around mid-December when the mental load is at its peak.

Whatever you do, don't let on that it's a chore: no one likes a grinch at Christmas. However, we would suggest that even though it is a lot of work (really, a lot. Have we mentioned how much work it is already?), it might just be worth the effort for the following reasons:

RITUALS AND FAMILY TRADITIONS

Rituals and traditions ultimately feed the spirit, grounding us in something timeless and deeply human. They connect us to our family and friends and contribute to a sense of belonging, and nowhere is this more so than at Christmastime. From the ritual of unpacking the tree decorations, each one bringing up an old memory, to digging out recipes you might only cook once a year, it is a time when we lean into the old, all of us in search of creating the magic we once felt and as a result creating new magic of our own.

IT'S COSY

Let's be honest, a big part of the joy of Christmas is that it is pretty, cosy and sparkly. Putting up the Christmas lights outside is time-consuming, tangly and sometimes dangerous. The reward is a month of coming home in the cold and dark to be greeted by warm, twinkling lights and the sight of the Christmas tree glowing through the window. The very idea of a Christmas tree is madness – but bringing a large, spiky tree into the house for absolutely no sane reason apart from 'it's tradition' is exactly what makes it special.

IT BUILDS COMMUNITY

Christmas is really all about other people, for better or for worse. Just like the food, we must gorge ourselves on the people in our lives throughout December until we can take no more. We sometimes need external factors to force us to get together because, let's face it, we would often opt out if we could. Not at Christmas though! Neighbourhood gatherings, carol concerts, children's nativities, a festive pub quiz: they exist because we need to feel part of something real, something that we can look back on one day and say 'do you remember when…?'

'Traditions connect us to family and friends.'

'Rituals feed the spirit, grounding us in something timeless and deeply human.'

Squash, walnut and Cheddar pithivier

SERVES 6
COOK TIME: 1 HOUR 30 MINUTES

1 medium butternut squash
3 tbsp olive oil
2 onions, peeled and diced
2 celery sticks, diced
15g sage, finely chopped
15g rosemary, finely chopped
200g walnuts
100g blanched almonds
100g mature Cheddar
2 x 500g blocks of puff pastry
1 egg, beaten
salt and pepper

A really great veggie centrepiece is often neglected, but here's a stunner. It's packed with festive nuts and herbs and would make a fabulous addition to your Christmas spread.

1. Heat the oven to 210°C/190°C fan.

2. Halve the squash and scoop out the seeds. Place the squash on a baking tray, drizzle with 1 tablespoon of the oil and scatter with a little salt, then roast for 45 minutes.

3. Meanwhile, heat the remaining 2 tablespoons of oil in a frying pan over a medium heat. Add the onions and cook for 15 minutes until softened. Add the celery, sage and rosemary and cook for another 5 minutes.

4. Spread the walnuts and almonds out on a baking tray and toast for 7 minutes until golden. Leave to cool slightly, then chop finely.

5. Scoop the flesh of the roasted squash into a large bowl. Tip in the onion mixture and chopped nuts, then grate in the Cheddar. Give everything a good mix, then season to taste with salt and pepper.

6. Line a large baking tray with baking parchment. Roll out one of the blocks of puff pastry to about 2mm thick. Cut out a 26cm diameter circle and place it on the lined tray. Score a circle about 3cm in from the edge, then spread the filling within this border. Brush the edge with the beaten egg.

7. Roll out the other puff pastry block to about 2mm thick, then lay it on top. Press the pastry edges together to seal them, then trim off the excess pastry around the outside. Press a fork around the edge to seal it neatly. Make a tiny hole in the centre, then gently score the pastry from the hole to the edge, curving it gently around to the right. Repeat until you have a pattern running all the way round.

8. Brush the pastry with the beaten egg, then chill in the fridge for 15 minutes. Brush again with egg, and return to the fridge for at least 30 minutes (or up to a day, if you like).

9. Heat the oven to 210°C/190°C fan. Bake for 30 minutes, then slice and serve.

Potato röstis with smoked salmon and crème fraîche

SERVES 4
COOK TIME: 20 MINUTES

500g Maris Piper potatoes
8 tbsp vegetable oil
8 tbsp crème fraîche
120g smoked salmon
½ small bunch of chives, finely chopped
1 lemon, cut into wedges
salt and pepper

A luxurious Christmas breakfast is the best way to begin the day and for the most decadent start, it has to be smoked salmon. Fancy these as canapés instead? Simply fry the röstis in smaller chunks.

1. Peel the potatoes, then grate them on the coarsest side of a box grater. Put the grated potato into a large bowl, cover with water and leave to soak for 20 minutes.

2. Drain the grated potato, then pop it into a clean tea towel. Twist the top so that the potato forms a ball in the middle, then squeeze out all the excess liquid over the sink.

3. Tip the potato into a clean bowl. Add 1 teaspoon of salt, then give everything a good mix. This is your rösti mixture.

4. Heat the oven to 150°C/130°C fan. Heat a large frying pan over a medium heat and add 4 tablespoons of the oil. Divide the rösti mixture in half and shape into golf-ball-sized handfuls (this quantity makes about 8 röstis). Add four handfuls to the hot oil and flatten them with a spatula. Cover the röstis with a piece of baking parchment, then place a heavy-bottomed pan or weight on top. Fry for about 5 minutes, then remove the parchment and weight and check that the undersides are crisp and golden (you may need to give them another minute or so).

5. Flip the röstis over and cook for 5 minutes on the other side, (without the weight on top). When they are cooked, remove from the pan and repeat with the remaining mixture. Keep the cooked röstis warm in the oven.

6. Plate up the röstis and top them with a dollop of crème fraîche, some smoked salmon, chives and a wedge of lemon. Crack over some black pepper and serve them up.

Sustainable gift-wrap ideas

If you are tired of buying wrapping paper just to see it end up in a black bin bag in the corner of the room and want a more environmentally friendly option, here are a few ideas that we love:

Reusable fabric: pretty tea towels, napkins or scraps of fabric can be used to wrap gifts (and can form part of the present itself). Secure them with string or ribbon that can be removed and used again.

Recycled newspaper: old newspaper can make excellent wrapping paper, especially when embellished with pretty sprigs or decorations from the outdoors. Just remember to choose your paper wisely, avoiding any traumatic headlines (sometimes trickier than you might think).

Upcycled maps, sheet music or pages of old books are a fun way to wrap presents, especially when teamed with colourful ribbons.

Cloth bags: turn old pillowcases into simple drawstring bags and put your gift in there. These can be used again and again.

'Christmas is all about other people. Like the food, we must gorge ourselves on the people we love throughout December.'

A final word from Jessica

We hope that you have enjoyed this wander around the Piglet in Bed home with us. You will have seen rooms in many colours, shapes and sizes, linked by the common threads of comfort and individuality.

Houses that feel warm and welcoming come from finding the confidence to stamp your own personal version of comfort and joy onto a space. This book is intended as a springboard from which you can draw inspiration for your own home – or you can simply disappear into the cosy world of Piglet in Bed as you turn the pages.

Floorboards scuffed from busy feet, a pile of books on the bedside table, a chipped bowl that holds many memories: there is so much beauty in the mess and imperfections of our homes if we choose to look for it.

Beautiful homes are made for living.

Index

A
accent colours 107
accessories, bathroom 107
aged possessions 12, 15
air drying 145
alcohol consumption 112, 148
ambience 148
armchairs 78, 80, 87, 90
art 96–101
art areas 89
artists 98
aubergine dip, smoked 138, 139

B
basil, potted 95, 142
bath mats 107
bath oils 111
bath salts 111
bathrooms 103–15
   accessories 107
   and colour 107
   entertainment for 112
   food for 112
baths 40, 108–12
beach picnics 132
bedrooms 17–43
   and the art of napping 36–8
   and colour 18, 21
   and eating in bed 24, 29
   and sleep 36–8, 40, and 43
   and wind-down routines 40
bed sheets, ironing 30
blankets, picnic 128
blinds 107
boredom 30
broccoli soup with Stilton

croutons 66, 67, 68–9
bubble bath 111

C
candles 111, 114, 117, 148, 157–8
centrepieces 158
charity shops 158
cheese
   broccoli soup with Stilton
   croutons 66, 67, 68–9
   creamed corn and tuna jacket
   potatoes 74, 75
   curried cheese on toast 28, 29
   picky bits 82, 83
   spinach and feta rolls 136, 137
   squash, walnut and Cheddar
   pithier 172, **173**
chicken pie 60, 61–2, **63**, 64, **65**
Christmas 92, 164–79
Christmas trees 167
cloakrooms 114–17
   showing off with 114
coasters 80
cocktails 148
colour
   accent 107
   and bathrooms 107
   and bedrooms 18, 21
   colour drenching 18
   colour theory 21
   colour-coding 54, 57
   cool 21, 95
   dark 107
   earthy 95
   energising 21
   and living rooms 95

   and mood 21
   nature-inspired 95
   neutrals 21, 95
   and pattern mixing 18, 157
   and tables aping 152, 157
   warm 21, 95
   and wood 92
comfort
comfort food 58
   and eating in bed 24
   and making a house a home 12
community 167
company 46, 48, 128
container gardening 95, 142–5
cookies 128
cosy atmospheres 158, 167
cotton 12, 95
creativity 30, 36, 58
   and cloakrooms 114, 117
   and gardening 124
   making space for 84, 89
   and picky bits platters 83
   and tablescapes 152
crème fraîche and potato röstis
   with smoked salmon **174**, 175
crockery 52, 128, 151, 157
croutons, Stilton 67
curried cheese on toast 28, 29
cutlery 157
cuttings 145

D
decanting 54, 55
decor, organic 157
dinner 40
dips 128

smoked aubergine 138, 139
drinks 148
du Maurier, Daphne, *Rebecca* 89
durability 12, 15

E
eggs 55, 132
emotions, and colour 21
Epsom salts 111
event picnics 132

F
face masks 111
family traditions 167
feta and spinach rolls 136, 137
fish
    creamed corn and tuna jacket potatoes 74, 75
    potato röstis with smoked salmon and crème fraîche 174, 175
flowers 151, 157, 158
food 40, 46–8, 55, 57
    broccoli soup with Stilton croutons 66, 67, **68–9**
    comfort food 58
    creamed corn and tuna jacket potatoes 74, 75
    dinner 40
    dips 128, **138**, 139
    eaten in the bath 112
    eating in bed 24, 29
    eating in the living room 80, 83
    pastry-based dishes 61–2, 128, 136, 137, 172, 173
    for picnics 128–32, **136**, 137, **138**, 139
    potato ranking 71
    potato röstis with smoked salmon and crème fraîche **174**, 175

smoked aubergine dip 138, 139
spillages 80
spinach and feta rolls 136, 137
squash, walnut and Cheddar pithivier 172, **173**
the ultimate chicken pie 60, 61–2, **63**, 64, **65**
when to serve 151
see also hosting
framing 96, 98, 101
freezing produce 145
fresh air 92
fridges 57
fruit 128, 157
fruit juice 55
furniture
    kitchen 52
    living room 78, 80, 87, 90

G
gardens 121–45
    indoor gardening 89
    picnicking 128–40
    and supermarket herbs 95, 142–5
gift wrap
    stations 87
    sustainable 176
glassware 128, 157, 158
grain patterns 92
green spaces 92, 95
greenhouses 89
guest lists 151

H
hanging art 101
herbs
    potted 95, 142
    storage 145
    supermarket 142–5
Hitchcock, Alfred 46

hobbies 30
    creating space for 84–9
hosting 147–79
    Christmas 164–79
    drinks 148
    guest lists 151
    and lighting 148
    and presentation skills 151
    spectrum of 148
    and tablescaping 152–62
    when to serve food 151
houseplants 95

I
imperfection, embracing 15, 107, 148, 180
individuality 12
inspiration 107
ironing
    sheets 30
    tablecloths 152

J
Jones, Bridget 148
joy 15
jute 95

K
kitchen dressers 52
kitchens 45–75
    and colour-coding 54, 57
    crimes 54–7
    and decanting 54, 55
    gravitational pull 46–8, 51, 78
    organisation 54–7
knitting corners 87
Kondo, Marie 15

L
label-makers 54, 55
lighting

and bedrooms 21, 24
and hosting 148
living room 80, 82, 87, 89, 92, 95
and neutrals 21
and wellbeing 92
see also natural light
linen 12, 21, 95, 107
living rooms 77–101
   and art 96–101
   colour palettes 95
   eating in 80, 83
   furniture 78, 80, 87, 90
   lighting 80, 82, 87, 89, 92, 95
   nooks 84–9
   rearranging 90
   and spillages 80
   and storage 80
   and TVs 78
   and welcoming the outside in 92–5
loofahs 111
luften concept 92

M
'me time' 108
milk 55
mint, propagation 145
mistakes, correction 21
mood 21, 92
Morris, William 15
mounts 101
mugs 52
music 148

N
napkins 152–8, 162
   the bow 162
   the knot 162
   the tie 162
napping, art of 36–8

natural light
   and bedrooms 21, 24
   and gardening 128, 132, 142, 145
   and living rooms 89, 92, 95
   and neutrals 21
   and sleep 82
   and wellbeing 92
natural materials 12, 92–5
nature, connecting with 124, 127
neutrals
   and bedrooms 21
   and living rooms 95
   and texture 21
newspaper gift wrap 176
nooks 84–9

O
organic decor 157
organic patterns 18
'outside in' concept 92–5

P
parks, picnics for 132
pastry-based dishes
   and picnics 128
   puff pastry 136, 137, 172, 173
   rough puff pastry 60, 61–2, 63, 64, 65
   spinach and feta rolls 136, 137
   squash, walnut and Cheddar pithivier 172, 173
   the ultimate chicken pie 60, 61–2, **63**, **64**, **65**
patterns
   geometric 18
   mixing 18, 152, 157
   organic 18
   palate-cleansers 18
   textural 18
   that share a common colour 18, 157
phones 40
physical activity 40, 92
pickles 58
picky bits, a guide to the perfect plate **82**, **83**
picnicking 128–40
   smoked aubergine dip **138**, **139**
   spinach and feta rolls **136**, **137**
pie, ultimate chicken 60, 61–2, **63**, **64**, **65**
pithivier, squash, walnut and Cheddar 172, **173**
place cards 157
place mats 157
plate chargers 157
potato
   broccoli soup with Stilton croutons **66**, **67**, **68–9**
   creamed corn and tuna jacket potatoes **74**, **75**
   potato röstis with smoked salmon and crème fraîche **174**, **175**
   ranking dishes 71
practicality 15
propagation 145
puff pastry
   spinach and feta rolls **136**, **137**
   squash, walnut and Cheddar pithivier 172, **173**

R
reading 24, 112
reading nooks 87
rearranging spaces 90
recipes
   broccoli soup with Stilton croutons **66**, **67**, **68–9**
   creamed corn and tuna jacket

potatoes **74**, 75
curried cheese on toast **28**, 29
picky bits plate **82**, 83
potato röstis with smoked salmon and crème fraîche **174**, 175
smoked aubergine dip **138**, 139
spinach and feta rolls **136**, 137
squash, walnut and Cheddar pithivier 172, **173**
the ultimate chicken pie 60, 61–2, **63**, 64, **65**
rituals 167
rough puff pastry, the ultimate chicken pie 60, 61–2, **63**, 64, **65**
rugs 80

S
salmon, potato röstis with smoked salmon and crème fraîche **174**, 175
sandwiches 128, 132
seating plans 151
secondhand goods 98, 158
sewing corners 87
sheets, ironing 30
shower curtains 107
showers 40
showing off 114
sleep 43
 the art of napping 36–8
 and natural light exposure 82
 wind-down routines 40
small spaces 107
smoked aubergine dip **138**, 139
snacks 112
 picky bits **82**, 83
 pre-dinner 151
 receptacles for 24

sofas 78, 80
soup, broccoli soup with Stilton croutons 66, **67**, 68–9
spillages 80
spinach
 broccoli soup with Stilton croutons 66, **67**, 68–9
 spinach and feta rolls **136**, 137
squash, walnut and Cheddar pithivier 172, **173**
Stewart, Martha 148
Stilton croutons 67
stone 95
storage, living room 80
stress reduction 108, 111, 112
style, discovering your 98
sustainable gift wrap 176
sweetcorn, creamed corn and tuna jacket potatoes **74**, 75
synthetic materials 12

T
table runners 152
tablecloths 152–8
tablescaping 152–62
 cosy atmospheres 158
 fun stuff 157
 functional stuff 157
 layering 152
 themes 152
 top tips 158
tableware 128, 157
 see also crockery
texture 18, 21, 95
thrift stores 158
toast, curried cheese on **28**, 29
tomatoes 132
towels 107, 111, 114
traditions, family 167
tuna and creamed corn jacket potatoes **74**, 75

TV 24, 30, 40, 78

U
upcycled gift wrap 176

W
walking 40
wallpapering 114
walnut, squash and Cheddar pithivier 172, **173**
wellbeing 92
wind-down routines 40
wine 112
Winslet, Kate 114
wood 92, 95
wool 12, 95
wrapping paper
 stations 87
 sustainable 176

Y
yogurt 55

INDEX

Acknowledgements

I'd like to take a moment to thank our Piglet in Bed team for making this dream possible. I get to wake up every day excited to bring a little bit of joy into people's homes and the pleasure of working with such a kind, thoughtful and hardworking group of people. From those colleagues who were with us in the early days packing orders in 'The Barn', all the way to those who have joined us more recently to help propel the business into its next stage of life, I'm eternally grateful.

Extra-special thanks to the wonderful Rhiannon, Georgie, Victoria and our talented illustrator, Sophia, who all played a central role in the creation of this book, and to my business partner Axel, who helped me take the kernel of idea and make Piglet in Bed a reality; I'm thankful every day for your unwavering support, dedication and steady hand.

About the authors

Rebecca Mason lives in London with her husband, three children, and their dog, River. After a career in finance, she stepped away to spend more time with her family and pursue her lifelong love of writing. When she isn't collaborating with her sister on lifestyle books, she's working on her debut novel. She's happiest by the sea, at a live gig or walking through the countryside with River in tow.

The recipes were created by **Sophie Wyburd**, a cook, food writer and presenter from South London. Formerly heading up the food team at Mob, you can now find her recipes in her debut cookbook *Tucking In*, and in her bestselling newsletter, *Feeder*. Her recipes have been featured in *The Times*, *Good Food*, *Sainsbury's Magazine* and the *Financial Times*, and she regularly appears on *Saturday Kitchen*. She also hosts sell-out supper clubs all over London, and co-hosts the *I'll Have What She's Having* and *A Bit of a Mouthful* podcasts.

Photography and styling credits

PHOTOGRAPHERS

Toby Mitchell
Mark Scott
Darcie Judson
Jaclyn Simpson
Lucy Laucht
Jon Day
Zoë Economides

Sophie Davidson
Valentina Concordia
Philippa Lawley-Barrett
Kate Davis
Stories Studio
Laura Edwards

WITH SPECIAL THANKS TO THE FOLLOWING PEOPLE FOR OPENING UP THEIR HOMES TO US

Ramona Jones — @monalogue
Uns Hobbs — @uns.hobbs_interiors
Genevieve Harris — @mrs_trufflepig
Sarah Laming — @ahometomakeyousmile
Lane Locations — @lane_locations
Nicola Huthwaite — @nicolahuthwaite
Jess Shah — @1_denison_house
The Flower Factory created by Kristin Perers — @kristinperers, available through lightlocations.com
Katharine Howard Style
Restaries, Suffolk
Vestry House

MODELS

Manon Steele
Jane McCall — @janemccallstudio
Freya Jenkin
Herbie Mensah — @greymodelagency
Stefanie Lange
Elena Forest

STYLISTS

Jessica McIntosh
Elkie Brown
Katie Phillipps

EBURY PRESS

UK | USA | Canada | Ireland | Australia | India | New Zealand | South Africa

Ebury Press is part of the Penguin Random House group of companies whose addresses can be found at global.penguinrandomhouse.com

Penguin Random House UK
One Embassy Gardens, 8 Viaduct Gardens, London SW11 7BW

penguin.co.uk
global.penguinrandomhouse.com

First published by Ebury in 2026
1

Text copyright © Piglet in Bed 2026
Photography © 2026 Darcie Judson pages 164, 165, 166, 168, 169, 170, 176, 177, 178; Lucy Laucht pages 10, 25, 31, 32, 39, 85, 89, 93, 192; Valentina Concordia pages 11, 13, 14, 22, 28, 33, 44, 49, 50, 53, 54, 56, 57, 59, 60, 63, 65, 66, 68, 69, 72, 73, 74, 79, 80, 82, 86, 88, 91, 94, 96, 97, 99, 100, 101, 105, 109, 113, 115, 118, 120, 122, 123, 124, 125, 126, 133, 136, 138, 140, 141, 143, 144, 146, 149, 150, 154, 156, 162, 163, 173, 174; Laura Edwards pages 37, 47; Toby Mitchell pages 84, 102, 106, 110, 116; Kate Davis pages 16, 19, 20, 23, 26, 27, 34, 153, 159, 160, 161, 162; Jon Day pages 9, 42; Zoë Economides page 119; Mark Scott page 181; Jaclyn Simpson pages 6, 180; Sophie Davidson pages 129, 130, 134, 138, 189; Philippa Lawley-Barrett pages 76, 81; Stories Studio page 41

The moral right of the author has been asserted.
No part of this book may be used or reproduced in any manner for the purpose of training artificial intelligence technologies or systems. In accordance with Article 4(3) of the DSM Directive 2019/790, Penguin Random House expressly reserves this work from the text and data mining exception.

Publishing Director: Elizabeth Bond
Project Editor: Imogen Fortes
Designer: Studio Polka
Production Controller: Percie Bridgewater

Colour origination by Altaimage Ltd
Printed and bound in China by C&C Offset Printing Co., Ltd

The authorised representative in the EEA is Penguin Random House Ireland, Morrison Chambers, 32 Nassau Street, Dublin D02 YH68.

A CIP catalogue record for this book is available from the British Library
ISBN 9781529964011

Penguin Random House is committed to a sustainable future for our business, our readers and our planet. This book is made from Forest Stewardship Council® certified paper.